Gérard de Nerval

GERARD DE NERVAL
PHOTOGRAPH BY NADAR
Ne m'attends pas ce soir, car la nuit
sera noire et blanche

GÉRARD DE NERVAL
A CRITICAL BIBLIOGRAPHY
1900 to 1967

by

JAMES VILLAS

with a preface by Jean Senelier

University of Missouri Studies Volume XLIX
University of Missouri Press
Columbia • Missouri

1/15/69   LJ

to Jacques Hardré
chevalier, maître, ami

Préface

UNE PRÉFACE À UNE BIBLIOGRAPHIE n'est pas courante car ce type d'ouvrage s'impose par son mérite propre, mais elle n'est pas inutile car il convient, de temps à autre, de remettre en mémoire que ce livre qui va servir à chaque instant a représenté pour son auteur, guetté à tout moment par un oubli ou une erreur, un effort continu pendant plusieurs années, une grande patience attentive et des soins minutieux.

La Bibliographie est une science ingrate, ceux qui consacrent leur temps et leur peine ne sont guère honorés que par une élite de spécialistes, mais, nous nous empressons de le dire, nul d'entre ces fervents des livres n'a jamais eu une préoccupation intéréssée en tête car ils trouvent une profonde satisfaction dans le travail de recherche qu'ils ont entrepris et qui leur vient de l'amour — le mot n'est pas trop fort pour l'écrivain ou le sujet qui a retenu leur attention.

Personnellement nous n'avons jamais écouté que notre plaisir dans nos investigations bibliographiques sur Jean-Jacques Rousseau et Nerval, nous avions même eu la naïveté outrecuidante d'avoir voulu cataloguer aussi tous les travaux consacrés à Jean-Jacques! Inutile de dire que nous dûmes vite battre en retraite devant l'énormité de la tâche; il en est resté environ trois mille fiches (une goutte d'eau!) objet d'un don à la Bibliothèque de l'Arsenal à l'intention d'un aventurier de la Bibliographie prêt à toutes les audaces.

Nous avons mesuré ici notre faiblesse en pensant aux géants d'autrefois: à la monumentale *Biblioteca universalis* de Conrad Gessner, aux 321 volumes manuscrits d'une *Bibliothèque universelle* écrits par le seul abbé Drouyn au XVIIe siècle, aux 40 volumes de l'*Orbis litteraris* de Savonarole et à bien d'autres encore.

Il était donc possible, dans le temps d'une vie humaine, de bâtir de tels temples bibliographiques, mais qui aurait la persévérance de se lancer maintenant dans de pareilles entreprises? La masse d'imprimés est si grande que nous voyons des équipes intellectuelles consacrer plusieurs années au recensement d'un sujet limité.

Dans le cas où ce sujet représente des dizaines de milliers de références les problèmes surgissent: comment distinguer, séparer, mettre en vedette, dans cet océan de livres, de brochures et d'articles, ce qui est essentiel par rapport à ce qui est secondaire? Quels critères de jugement faut-il adopter? Comment éviter l'arbitraire (un article de trois pages peut être plus important qu'un livre de trois cents)?

Tout ceci oblige donc soit à cataloguer sans distinction, et le consulteur est perdu dans cette forêt, soit à établir une codification typographique où mieux, une notice plus ou moins succincte pour chaque titre, mais alors l'ouvrage prend une dimension considérable restreignant les possibilités de son édition et par suite, de son achat.

Revenons à des hauteurs plus accessibles, nous voulons dire ici tout le grand bien que nous pensons et féliciter nos amis américains pour leur *French VII* (et *VI*) *Bibliography* du French Institute de New-York car c'est là un travail excellent, très bien conçu et réalisé dont nous n'avons pas l'équivalent en France, nous souhaitons qu'il y soit loué comme il le mérite.

Lorsque nous avons entrepris à partir de 1953 de réunir les matériaux d'une Bibliographie de Gérard de Nerval nous n'avons eu la possibilité matérielle et le temps de lire qu'une petite fraction des travaux consacrés à notre auteur, aussi nous sommes particulièrement heureux de présenter ici le remarquable essai de M. James Villas qui est le complément nécessaire de notre propre effort. Son livre est ce *guide* obligatoire des étudiants et des chercheurs quand la bibliographie d'un sujet devient abondante, il permet de s'y orienter et d'y trouver ce que l'on cherche soit du point de vue des idées, soit du point de vue des faits.

Rédiger une sélection bibliographique de plusieurs centaines de titres et faire suivre chacun d'eux d'un commentaire analytique n'est pas un travail de tout repos et nous devons féliciter M. James Villas de l'avoir fait; il nécessite d'abord beaucoup de persévérance mais surtout le goût et le sens du discernement, enfin l'art de transcrire fidèlement la pensée de chaque auteur sous une forme succincte et claire.

Tous ces impératifs sont pleinement satisfaits par M. Villas dans son livre qui nous apporte ainsi une bien utile contribution pour l'étude de Nerval. Nous souhaitons vivement que son Essai soit transcrit dans notre langue car il ne faut pas se dissimuler que les ébauches tentées dans ce sens, et sans commune mesure, par M. R.M. Albérès en 1955, par M. Léon Cellier en 1957 (récemment aussi par M. Alfred DuBruck) nous laissaient sur notre faim et devaient être renouvelées. C'est chose faite grâce à M. James Villas.

Son travail nous montre combien sont nombreux les motifs d'investigation pour les chercheurs dans une vie et une oeuvre paradoxales: peu d'écrits, une imagination limitée, une existence errante assez grise, pénible, traversée de rares moments de bonheur et pourtant, issue d'une alchimie mystérieuse naît une richesse unique de ton, de style et de résonance intérieure au-delà des mots. La Bibliographie nervalienne nous apporte la preuve d'une variété de thèmes, de leur profondeur, toutes choses restées ignorées pendant plus d'un quart de siècle; cette découverte de la mythologie personnalisée de Nerval nous paraît être l'excellent signe de notre curiosité, ainsi que de notre attachement pour des valeurs traditionnelles, en dehors du rationalisme, mais dont la présence toujours vivante est irrécusable.

JEAN SENELIER

Paris, 14 janvier 1968

Contents

Introduction

THIS BIBLIOGRAPHICAL STUDY of Gérard de Nerval is the first attempt on a large scale to analyze and appraise the most important books and articles written on Nerval during the twentieth century. Several studies during the past few years have included evaluative surveys of modern Nerval scholarship, but none of these has afforded anything like adequate coverage of the vast amount of critical material that has appeared since the turn of the century. In 1956, Léon Cellier devoted the final chapter of his superb *Gérard de Nerval, l'homme et l'oeuvre* (64)* to general trends in Nerval research, citing the outstanding scholars in the field and commenting on their work. The following year, Professor Cellier surveyed again the best critical works on the author in his brief but informative *Où en sont les recherches sur Gérard de Nerval* (65), proposing, at the same time, an extremely valuable program of research. The first chapter of Raymond Jean's *Nerval par lui-même* (184) of 1964 considered Nerval criticism, but it is too cursory to be really useful. The *"Etat présent* of Nerval Studies" in Alfred DuBruck's *Gérard de Nerval and the German Heritage* (113) of 1965 is a thirty-page commentary on studies devoted primarily to the German influences on Nerval. The most recent contribution is my own "Present State of Nerval Studies: 1957 to 1967" (381), which offers as complete a critical outline as possible of the most interesting and significant studies to appear on Nerval since the publication of Cellier's work in 1957.

Since, from the beginning, I have worked in close affiliation with M. Jean Senelier, the present work is intended as a companion vol-

*Throughout this volume, the numerical references in parentheses are the numbers of individual items listed in the critical bibliography.

ume to his *Gérard de Nerval: essai de bibliographie* (351) of 1959, as well as to his forthcoming *complément*, which has been scheduled for publication by Nizet in 1968. I pretend in no way to offer a complete critical coverage of all 1,222 secondary items in Senelier's 1959 bibliography, for many listings are obviously of little value or are almost impossible to locate. Instead, for the period up to 1959, I have commented only on those items (approximately one third of Senelier's references) which represent the finest available Nerval scholarship or which, because of ambiguous titles, might raise some questions as to content. For the period between 1959 and 1967, I have attempted to discuss every important item I was able to consult. Had M. Senelier not made the decision to bring his bibliography up to date, I would have offered (in an appendix) a complete listing of primary and secondary material from 1959 to the present.

My decision to limit the critical coverage to the sixty-seven-year period was reached when M. Jean Richer informed me of his intention to publish in 1967 or 1968 a *Nerval par les témoins de sa vie* (Minard). This study, which will supposedly treat the major commentaries and criticism on Nerval from 1830 to approximately 1900, should complement the bibliography I have prepared for the modern era.

Some readers will notice immediately that I have not dealt with the various editions of Nerval's works. Those interested in critical commentary on any primary material are referred to the astute introductions in Senelier's two bibliographies.

There will be, of course, other readers who might question certain items I have estimated (or have not estimated) to be important contributions to Nerval research. My only defenses in this matter are my personal taste and any sensitivity I might have developed toward the literary criticism of an author to whom I have devoted a number of years. There are, without doubt, respectable articles, perhaps even books, that have escaped my perusal. And, admittedly, there are a few items that, after the most intensive efforts, I was simply unable to consult.* Furthermore, since I have left the problem of editions to M. Senelier, there exist most surely many enlightened prefaces and introductions which are not considered here. In a work of this nature many lines, unfortunately, must be drawn.

*For example, Karlheinz Stierle's *Dunkelheit und Form in Gérard de Nervals Chimères* (München: W. Fink, 1967).

This volume is divided into two parts. The first, entitled "Gérard de Nerval in the Twentieth Century," is an evaluative chronological discussion of modern trends in Nerval scholarship. Although I felt it necessary to comment briefly on the period before 1900, the emphasis in this introductory essay is definitely on the critical material that has appeared during the past six and a half decades, and particularly on that from 1930 to 1967. This section indicates also the pressing need for a more thorough investigation of Nerval's romanticism, his correspondence, his dramatic *feuilletons*, his minor poetry and prose, and his style.

The second part is the critical bibliography of almost four hundred items covering numerous aspects of Nerval's life and work. Since the primary objective in a book of this type is utility, I decided to arrange the entries alphabetically by author and to consider the chronological development of research in the introductory essay on Nerval in the twentieth century. In addition to being listed alphabetically, the entries are numbered consecutively and are referred to by number throughout the entire volume. Each item is accompanied by a concise résumé of subject matter and, in most cases, by a brief critical evaluation. Reviews of many entries are cited after the commentary and are identified with small alphabetic characters.

To this part is appended a short listing of unpublished or unfinished doctoral theses both in this country and in Europe. Although it is virtually impossible to offer definite data on items of this nature, as it is equally impossible to learn of every thesis that has been or is presently being written on Nerval, I hope this section might be of some use to certain readers. It is also my hope that future *nervaliens* will inform me about their work.

The Index, which refers to the numbered items of the Bibliography and the appended listing, should facilitate location of material and be especially useful to anyone interested in studies on such matters as literary influences, themes, poetic structure, and the like.

I take this opportunity to acknowledge my indebtedness to M. Jean Senelier for his authoritative advice and generous assistance in the assemblage of material; to Messrs. Léon Cellier, Alfred DuBruck, John W. Kneller, Jean Richer, and Professor Norma Rinsler of King's College London, distinguished Nervalians, all of whom have responded to my many inquiries and expressed a continuing interest in the project; to Professor Bonner Mitchell of the University of Missouri for his kind patience in reading the final manuscript and for his invaluable suggestions; and, finally, to Professor Alfred G. Engstrom, who was my master at the University of North Carolina, who first introduced me to Gérard de Nerval, and who instilled in me the beauty of great literature.

J. V.

Columbia, Missouri
October, 1967

I. Gérard de Nerval in the Twentieth Century

The Legend of Nerval

FEW SCHOLARS OF FRENCH LITERATURE would contest today the distinguished position of Gérard de Nerval in the great hierarchy of French poets. His reputation is now firmly established, and few could deny the considerable influence his example has exerted on the literary consciousness of the twentieth century. Unlike Victor Hugo and Baudelaire, however, whose creative work received recognition during their day and whose fame has continued to grow during our era, Nerval was forced to wait nearly half a century before coming into his deserved inheritance.

One might assert justifiably that Gérard's work was doomed initially by its very nature, an artistic brilliance that transcended the concept of Romanticism and that consequently was both misunderstood and unappreciated by the poet's contemporaries (with the exception of Baudelaire, who credited Nerval with possessing "une intelligence brillante, active, lumineuse"). To most of his fellow Romantics, and to the public at large, Gérard de Nerval was little more than a talented journalist, whose extraordinary interest in dream and fantasy led to insanity and ultimately to suicide in the Rue de la Vieille Lanterne. Even Jules Janin and Gautier, two of his closest companions, proved incapable of comprehending the unique merit of Gérard's art. For these two, as well as for Dumas père, Mirecourt, Houssaye, and most of the other Romantics, Nerval was and remained "le doux Gérard" and "le fol délicieux." One need only read Janin's 1841 commentary, published in the *Journal des Débats* on the occasion of Nerval's first internment in the asylum. Here Gérard is described as

> . . . un de ces jeunes gens sans fiel, sans ambition, sans envie, à qui pas un bourgeois ne voudrait donner en mariage même sa fille borgne et bos-

> sue. . . . Il vivait au jour le jour, acceptant avec reconnaissance, avec
> amour, chacune des belles heures de la jeunesse, tombées du sein de Dieu.
> Il avait été riche un instant, mais par goût, par passion, par instinct, il
> n'avait pas cessé de mener la vie des plus pauvres diables. Seulement il
> avait obéi plus que jamais au caprice, à la fantaisie, à ce merveilleux vaga-
> bondage dont ceux-là qui l'ignorent disent de mal.

Or Gautier's romantic exaggerations in the preface to the first edition
of *Aurélia ou le rêve et la vie*:

> Nous avons retrouvé les derniers feuillets de cet étrange travail . . . dans
> les poches du mort. Il le portait avec lui comptant achever la phrase inter-
> rompue. . . . Mais la main a laissé tomber le crayon, et le rêve a tué la
> vie, l'équilibre maintenu jusque-là s'était rompu: cet esprit si charmant,
> si ailé, si lumineux, si tendre, s'est évaporé à jamais. . . .

Necrological articles written by Francis Wey, Félix Mornand, Joseph
Méry, and Dumas are of the same general nature, expressing pity, fascination, devotion, but never supreme admiration of a man who was
above all an artist. Only in September of 1861, six years after Gérard's
suicide, does Charles Asselineau publish in the *Revue Fantaisiste* an
article that at least attempts to deaden the echoes of the Rue de la
Vieille Lanterne and to investigate an aspect of Nerval's poetic personality:

> Supposez cet homme initié aux correspondances de la mystique, aux sub-
> tilités de la gnose; donnez-lui la connaissance du Magisme et de la Kab-
> bale; nous franchissons un pas.

Thus, there is little reason to doubt that Gérard's posthumous reputation as a "romantique mineur" was due more directly than indirectly
to the failure of his contemporaries to recognize the true value of his
work and to realize the full intensity of his poetic message. Baudelaire
alone recognized Gérard's individuality and insight, by acknowledging
him as his "frère maudit." The author of *Les Fleurs du Mal* apparently
found in Gérard's work certain artistic means by which he could transcend the world of reality and enter into "la vie antérieure." Although
the two poets were never intimate friends, and although Baudelaire
never wrote at any length on Gérard, the complementary tenets of
their work attest to what the twentieth century has discovered to have
been a close spiritual rapport.

    The "legend" of Gérard de Nerval was perpetuated throughout
most of the second half of the nineteenth century by the notes and

commentaries of such figures as Georges Bell, Maxime du Camp, and Audebrand, all of whom insisted on accumulating petty, sordid facts on the poet's strange life and none of whom made any sincere effort to enlighten the public on Gérard's work. As a result, much emphasis was placed on the eccentric man and little attention was given to the artist. While Michel Lévy published six volumes of the *Oeuvres complètes* between 1867 and 1877, Gustave Lanson (one of the few writers of manuals to even mention the poet) accorded Nerval the following statement in the ninth edition of the *Histoire de la littérature française*: "1828. Gérard de Nerval, le *Faust* de Goethe." An interesting contrast would certainly be the eleven pages devoted to the poet in 1963 by Lagarde-Michard.

Many critics today have convinced themselves (and the public) that Gérard's modern popularity was due initially to the overwhelming influence he exercised on the Symbolists and their movement during the 1870's and 1880's. This possibility is highly exaggerated and, to some degree, actually false. While Rimbaud and Mallarmé were perhaps acquainted with *Sylvie*, *Aurélia*, and *Les Chimères*, there is little reason to believe that they would have attempted to fashion their ideas on literary symbolism after the works of a practically unknown "mineur," who, like the others of his school, was judged as an exponent of Romanticism; and, as Léon Cellier has so justifiably asserted, "Le romantisme était considéré comme . . . le compendium de la 'stupidité' du XIXe siècle." Furthermore, it should be emphasized that the "symbolism" (and "surrealism") of Nerval far transcended the literary artifices employed by most of the later poets. The absolute authenticity of his poetic vision, the simplicity and humility of his experience, and the lucidity of his mystical *connaissance* relate only obliquely to the proposals made by such a poet as Mallarmé. In reality, Gérard de Nerval anticipated a literary movement, the basic principles of which were inherent in his work; but his indirect participation in the movement was by no means realized by writers and scholars until nearly a half century after his death.

Ironically enough, the first critic to recognize and point out Nerval's literary importance was the British writer Arthur Symons, who, in 1899, published his important study on *The Symbolist Movement in Literature* (London: W. Heinemann). This study was and remains of paramount significance. Writing from the perspective of

Symbolist experience, Symons presented Nerval not as a raving lunatic but as a man with an inner vision whose work demonstrated the symbol as an indispensable artistic device and whose poetic discipline and control allowed him to transcend the realm of human reality. That Symons' judgments were limited to *Sylvie, Aurélia,* and *Les Chimères* alters in no way the solid impact of his commentary on both his French- and English-speaking successors. He showed that Gérard had introduced a new aesthetics into art, a poetic beauty and language that "uncovered the hidden links of divergent things in a sensitive unity of nature" (p. 37).

1900–1930

The first three decades of the twentieth century witnessed the gradual evolution of Nerval's literary popularity. The earliest important treatment of the poet in France was Julia Cartier's *Un Intermédiaire entre la France et L'Allemagne* (58), published in 1904 and based on the Michel Lévy edition of Nerval's writings and a certain number of unpublished texts. Although the thesis contained many errors and misconceptions, as well as a generally distorted view of Gérard's literary importance, it opened the way for future scholarly and public interest in a figure who had been all but forgotten in France. Within the next two years there appeared two other items on Nerval's Germanism, Ernest-Charles' "Gérard de Nerval et l'Allemagne" (126) and Marcel Breuillac's "Hoffmann en France" (52), both of which, if nothing else, introduced the poet's name to the reading public. Gauthier-Ferrières' biography of 1906, *Gérard de Nerval: la vie et l'oeuvre* (146), served to reinforce Gérard's impression but also helped to establish a regrettable tradition in which Nerval would be viewed (as he is still by many) more in terms of his Romantic "legend" than as a serious, creative artist.

This myth was temporarily stifled in 1914 by Aristide Marie's monumental *Gérard de Nerval, le poète et l'homme* (222), the publication of which failed to impress Nerval upon the consciousness of readers confronted with the possibility of war. However, with the end of the First World War in 1918, this critical biography was widely recognized, and it served as the basis for future critical interest in and appreciation of the poet. Although Marie's work suffered in part from his almost uncontrolled enthusiasm for Gérard, and although certain of its facts and critical opinions have been and will continue to be contested, Marie's data are reasonably exact and his scholarship is sound. It is highly probable that this early biography (reprinted in 1955) will continue for many years to be respected as a standard work on the subject.

Perhaps the most significant single influence on Nerval's rise to public fame was an article by Marcel Proust, published in 1920 in the *Nouvelle Revue Française*. Writing "A propos du 'style' de Flaubert" (278), Proust praised Gérard de Nerval as "assurément un des trois ou quatre plus grands écrivains du XIXe siècle" (p. 86) and stated that he partially discovered his own poetic method (or "ce procédé de brusque transition") in Chateaubriand's *Mémoires d'Outre-Tombe* and in Nerval's *Les Filles du Feu*. His tribute to Nerval in *Le Temps retrouvé* as an "ancestor" of the process of involuntary memory was of still greater import:

> Un des chefs-d'oeuvres de la littérature française, *Sylvie*, de Gérard de Nerval, a, tout comme le livre des *Mémoires d'Outre-Tombe* relatif à Combourg, une sensation du même genre que le goût de la madelaine et "la gazouillement de la grive."

Proust was the first to speak of Gérard as "ce grand génie," a compliment that would not go unrecognized by the Surrealists and André Breton, who, in the *Manifeste du surréalisme* of 1924, made the following declaration: "Il semble en effet que Nerval posséda à merveille *l'esprit* dont nous nous réclamons." By 1925 Nerval had definitely come into his deserved estimation, and the way had opened for a more lucid interpretation of the poet and his work.

The year 1926 is still another bench mark in the evolution of Nerval scholarship. To complement the three separate editions of *oeuvres complètes* by Champion, Bernouard, and le Divan (all of which remained incomplete), Aristide Marie published his *Bibliographie des Oeuvres de Gérard de Nerval* (221), the first formal attempt to list Nerval's works and the critical studies devoted to him before 1926. Containing 345 references to primary works and 191 secondary items, the bibliography, though faulty in many areas, remained the most valuable tool for research until the publication of the Senelier bibliography in 1959 (351). Pierre Audiat's *L'Aurélia de Gérard de Nerval* (7) of 1926 was equally important, for it demonstrated a method of literary interpretation of text that was to serve (or should have served) as a model for future studies on Nerval. Discussing chronologically how each of the poet's works represents a stage in the gradual development of a single, personal myth, Audiat contended that "*Aurélia* n'est que le dernier état d'une oeuvre qui a revêtu successivement plusieurs formes" (p. 28). Unfortunately, his approach had little effect on his French contemporaries, who, for the most part, continued to distort both the image of Nerval and his position in French letters. While the two major advocates of *poésie pure*, Henri Bremond (51) and René Lalou (200), left much to be desired in their appraisal of Gérard's poetic talents, René Bizet in 1928 (38) and Henri Clouard in 1929 (82) produced two utterly mediocre biographies, both of which presented Nerval as the "hero poet." Helen Merz's *Traum und Wirklichkeit bei Gérard de Nerval* (232) of 1929 deserves recognition. Unlike most of the material on Nerval being published in France during the late twenties, this stylistic analysis concentrated on the primary texts and showed, in the tradition of P. Audiat, how the texts demonstrated the writer's gradual recession into the poetic dreamworld.

1930–1940

The decade of the 1930's saw a major change in critical attitude toward Nerval. Whereas the scholars of the two previous decades had been generally content merely to establish the identity of the mythical poet, writers now began to profit from the devoted research of Marie and Audiat and insisted on a more thorough investigation of Gérard's individual works. Less and less interest was expressed in the purely biographical, and more emphasis was placed on the relationship between the poet's life and his creative art. Henri Strentz's *Gérard de Nerval, son oeuvre* (365) of 1933 succeeded in breaking away from the "legend" and analyzed seriously parts of a poetic work that Strentz felt "gagne chaque année de nouveaux et plus attentifs lecteurs" (p. 76). Six years later, Kléber Haedens, in his *Gérard de Nerval, ou la sagesse romantique* (171), made one of the first efforts to distinguish Nerval's Romanticism from that of his contemporaries:

> . . . Pour Nerval créer, c'est remonter aux sources de l'existence, c'est porter le faisceau de lumière au sein de la plus dense nuit. (p. 55)

Haedens' contribution was important, for it recognized Gérard as a poet who, like Baudelaire, had transcended artistically the superficialities of his Romantic environment.

In 1936 Otto Weise published a dissertation entitled *Gérard de Nerval, Romantik und Symbolismus* (388), in which he discussed the various aspects of Nerval's work that might link him with later literary movements. The study was practically devoid of biographical matter and focused its maximum concentration on the primary works. In addition to being one of the first to acknowledge the affinities between Nerval and Baudelaire (in Chapter IV), Weise provided a partial revision of the Marie bibliography of 1926 and a list of publications on Nerval in English.

While these critics were attempting to place Nerval in a more clearly defined historical perspective, others were delving into the individual works and introducing topics that were to seize the imagination of future Nervalians. René Daumal's article of 1930, "Nerval le nyctalope" (105), investigated "le monde intermédiaire" of *Aurélia* and showed how strongly the concepts of the *tout* and the *double* inhered in Nerval's thought and how each allowed the poet that interior elevation so necessary both for the artistic creation and for an ultimate understanding of and victory over death. Daumal's pioneer study in this area provided footing, without a doubt, for the later treatments of Gérard's esotericism and occultism by Rolland de Renéville, Georges Le Breton, and Jean Richer.

Nerval's important role in the development of the French *chanson populaire* was first pointed out in Julien Tiersot's *La Chanson populaire et les écrivains romantiques* (370) of 1931, a work to which Guichard (165) was later to turn for his more enlightened commentary on the subject. The following year Jean-Marie Carré (56) stimulated interest in the *Voyage en Orient* by stating that "il y a, dans [le] récit, plus de poésie que de vérité" (p. 17). Classifying the *Voyage en Orient* as perhaps Nerval's most creative work and the very best of its type in the Romantic period, Carré studied in detail the artistic development of the piece and demonstrated how the poet's distortion of fact and reality allowed him to seize upon "le prestige et la durée des créations éternelles de l'art" (p. 17). Equally influential was Jean Boucoiran's *La Sylvie de Gérard de Nerval* (45), published in the next year. This book, the first serious study of the work most admired by Proust, analyzed the *nouvelle* as a work of creative art and inspired five years later what is still considered today one of the most admirable commentaries on the element of Time in *Sylvie*: Georges Poulet's "*Sylvie* ou la pensée de Nerval" (275).

In 1934 the third in the chronological line of great *nervaliens*, François Constans, published his first article on Nerval, "Artémis ou les fleurs du désespoir" (89). In this exhaustive exegesis of the sonnet "Artémis" the author not only pointed out the very definite influence of Hoffmann on Nerval's imagination but also demonstrated a method of literary explication that would serve as a model for years to come. Though extremely complex (as are all of his critical writings on Nerval), Constans's analysis considered each element of the poem in terms of imagery, symbolism, biography, and external influences, all with the ultimate intention of reconciling the poet with his art. Above all, Constans did not limit his view to the single poem but strove to interpret the sonnet in the light of Nerval's other works.

This example of sound scholarship must surely have inspired Jeanine Moulin, who, in 1937, published *Les Chimères de Gérard de Nerval* (245). Preceded by a comprehensive introduction, this line-by-line elucidation of all *Les Chimères* is a glowing attempt to study the symbolic value of each sonnet and to bring into focus the unity of the collection. Moulin was fortunately of the opinion that "les explications . . . ne constituent . . . que des points de repère qui permettent tout au plus de se diriger à travers les passages obscurs" (p. lii). In view of the fact that she had access only to the Michel Lévy edition of Nerval's works, one cannot justly condemn her failure to consider all the variants and to reach a more definite conclusion as to the meaning behind the over-all structure of the collection. This edition was and remains extremely useful to anyone interested in Nerval's greatest poetry.

Rolland de Renéville's inclusion of Nerval as a mystic poet in his *L'Expérience poétique* (334) of 1938 can be credited to no other than Albert Béguin, who spent most of his life reading Nerval and who was writing about the poet at the time of his death in 1957. Béguin's first study in 1936, *Gérard de Nerval, suivi de Poésie et Mystique* (24), was devoted to *Aurélia* and suggested ideas that were to revolutionize trends in critical approach to Gérard's work. Béguin first of all saw *Aurélia*, not as the clinical portrayal of a lunatic, but as a well-formed work of art, composed by a man who, in his attempt to attain spiritual light, relates "l'histoire d'une lutte titanique, qui s'achève par un triomphe" (p. 9). Second, he pointed out the three spiritual levels on which the *récit* is constructed, levels that blend artistically to create "le drame de la connaissance" and that allow the poet to transcend, by love and charity, "l'insoutenable existence du mal" (pp. 129–30). That numerous scholars have since contested Béguin's interpretation and accused him of over-emphasizing Gérard's mystical nature proves simply that they either have not read his work carefully or have arbitrarily insisted on rejecting a sound, plausible explanation of the Nervalian experience in favor of a "new," superficial one. In 1939, Béguin's method of analysis employed in his study of *Aurélia* was applied to Nerval's poetry in *L'Ame romantique et le rêve* (21), a work of paramount importance in the study of the influence of German Romantic poetry on French Romanticism. Analyzing the role of dream in Nerval's transfiguration of reality into personal myth, the critic introduced a subject that had hardly been touched upon and that would influence the opinions of readers and scholars alike for the next two decades. Out of print for many years, the book was reprinted eventually by Corti in 1960.

1940–1950

The decade of the 1940's, and especially the period immediately following the Second World War, produced a significant amount of criticism on Nerval. Inspired greatly by the ideas of Béguin (whose collected essays on the poet were published by Corti in 1945 [22]), scholars began to devote their attention to the more intricate artistic qualities of Gérard's major works (*Sylvie, Aurélia, Les Chimères,* and *Voyage en Orient*), but they continued to neglect his minor prose pieces and his theatre. At a quick glance, it appears that in this period the primary efforts of Nerval criticism were aimed in three directions: the investigation of possible occult sources, the psychological interpretation of texts, and the intricate exegeses of major works. A good, well-documented edition of the *oeuvres* was in constant demand and would have expedited considerably the needed research on the minor works. Up until 1952, Nerval enthusiasts generally had access only to editions of the major works, and most of these left much to be desired in completeness and in critical annotation.

During the war years, Nerval's growing reputation and appeal were almost totally dependent on the work of scholars in America. The two most outstanding studies were by Edouard Roditi and S. A. Rhodes. Roditi's enlightened article of 1944, "Memory, Art and Death: Proust and Nerval" (333), fulfilled the need for a sound comparative study of the two authors, and it retains today the merit of being the only significant study devoted exclusively to this important subject. The author's conclusion is worth citing:

> For Proust, the real material event in the past becomes . . . revived and transfigured by memory when some analogous but less real and . . . less ideal experience in the present reveals the otherwise elusive substance which these two accidental manifestations have in common. It is this quality of realism which . . . drove him to seek concrete achievement in art rather than the more transcendental dreams which misled Nerval, through bright illusion and dark disillusionment, to final suicide. (p. 196)

In the same year Rhodes brought to the attention of the critics Nerval's only novel, *Le Marquis de Fayolle*, in a short article entitled "Gérard de Nerval's Unfinished Novel" (287). His consideration of the novel as "an imaginatively conceived work that bears on almost every page the stamp of [Gérard's] temperament" (p. 299) was impressive; it helped inspire Raymond Jean (185) in 1955 to analyze in greater detail what many consider an artistic prose work.

Before 1946–1947, when Camille Ducray (118) and Elvira Salvi (340) published two critical biographies of the poet and when Anna Balakian included Nerval in her *Literary Origins of Surrealism* (11), Georges Le Breton had produced remarkable results in his investigation of Nerval's readings in the esoteric and occult sciences. In his two long articles of 1945, "La Clé des *Chimères*: l'alchimie" (208) and "L'Alchimie dans *Aurélia*" (207), Le Breton demonstrated the importance of alchemy and the Tarot in two of the poet's major works and insisted on the over-all influence of Court de Gebelin's *Monde primitif* . . . and Dom Pernety's *Fables égyptiennes et grecques*. . . . Whether or not his theories were entirely well founded, the reaction to Le Breton's discoveries was no less than sensational (and certainly excessive), to the point that, from 1945 on, numerous Nervalians began to analyze all the poet's art in terms of alchemical symbolism, astrology, the Cabbala, Manichaeism,

Gnosticism, etc., etc. The one figure who adhered generally to the "new doctrines" but who refused to accept blindly the findings of another scholar was Jean Richer, without doubt the most eminent of all *nervaliens*. His first work on Nerval, *Gérard de Nerval et les doctrines ésotériques* (303) of 1947, developed and added to the findings of Le Breton. Whatever one's opinion of the book, one certainly cannot deny that Richer's scholarship is sound and demonstrates a rare devotion to the poet and his work. If nothing else, one cannot fail to be amazed at the sheer mass of accumulated esoteric data that have undoubtedly influenced trends in Nerval scholarship and opened up a new universe for those interested in esoteric aspects of the poet's work.

The following year, 1948, the journal *Cahiers du Sud* devoted a special section of one issue to Gérard de Nerval. Raymond Jean's sensitive study of "Le Vert Paradis de Gérard" (188) was complemented beautifully by François Constans' "Sur la pelouse de Mortefontaine" (100), which dealt with artistic place-setting, not only in *Sylvie*, but in all Gérard's later works. In "Les Pouvoirs de la femme selon Nerval et Breton" (57) Michel Carrouges commented on the animation of Nerval's celestial universe and demonstrated how the eternal Feminine evolves into a totally religious being, a conciliator between man and nature:

> Sous cet étrange syncrétisme qui unit en une seule vision toutes les femmes de la terre, les mères, les amantes et les prestigieuses figures féminines des mythologies et des religions, il est aisé de reconnaître une fabuleuse incarnation de l'éternel féminin. (p. 421)

A fourth item, Béguin's "Nerval en 1949" (26), anticipated the poet's rising popularity the following year and during the decade of the 1950's. As always, Béguin maintained his beliefs that Nerval's art is complete within itself and that studies of occult and esoteric influences are virtually useless insofar as an appreciation of the poetic experience is concerned.

It is rather surprising that Béguin endorsed L.-H. Sébillotte's *Le Secret de Gérard de Nerval* (348), an extremely controversial publication of 1948 that placed Nerval's "impuissance sexuelle" at the center of his neurosis and mental conflict. Unfortunately, most of Sébillotte's theories were preconceived and were rarely the result of close investigation of Nerval's works. However, this attempt to "psychoanalyze" the poet opened up still another area for research and has led to some interesting and worthwhile studies. In 1949 Charles Mauron questioned Sébillotte's thesis in his "Nerval et la psycho-critique" (229), in which he demanded a more careful analysis of the major texts. An attentive reading of *Aurélia, Les Chimères*, the letters to Jenny Colon, and *Léo Burckart* revealed personal elements that allowed the critic not only to define persuasively the psychological trauma that so affected the poet's life and work, but also to depict the outstanding mother image and the theme of the *double*. Furthermore, his examination of Nerval's esotericism restored a sensible perspective to such studies. Mauron's approach was sound and was to exercise substantial influence on succeeding critics, who were to concern themselves with the intricate psychology of Nerval's later works, particularly *Aurélia*.

1950–1960

By 1950 Gérard de Nerval was recognized as a major French Romantic, and his name appeared not only in anthologies of French literature but on the "A paraître" lists of the most distinguished publishing houses in France. In 1952 Gallimard included Volume I of Nerval's *Oeuvres* in its "Bibliothèque de la Pléiade" series, and in 1956 Volume II accompanied the Richer-Béguin revision of the first volume. Garnier's two-volume edition of the *Oeuvres* in 1958, edited by Henri Lemaître, was still another welcome gift to Nervalians who, up to this decade, had been forced to refer to incomplete, poorly documented, and, in many cases, incorrect texts. With the publication of these two editions, scholars had easy access to reasonably well established major texts as well as to most of the minor ones. Once these editions were made readily available to the public, interest and enthusiasm in Nerval increased sensationally, while critical books and articles more than doubled in number.

The decade of the fifties produced numerous items of a critical-biographical nature. Jean Richer's important *Gérard de Nerval* (301) of 1950 provided over a hundred pages of biography and well-documented commentary before suggesting various levels on which the poet's texts might be analyzed. The following year S. A. Rhodes published the only complete biography in English (286) and attempted (somewhat unsuccessfully) to interpret Nerval's works in the light of autobiographical elements. While R.-M. Albérès, in his *Gérard de Nerval* (3) of 1955, succeeded quite admirably in defining the close relationship between Gérard's life and his poetic creativity, and Eduardo Aunos y Perez developed his biography, *Gérard de Nerval et ses énigmes* (8), around the concept of the "descente aux enfers," Jean Béchade-Labarthe studied in as much detail as possible the *Origines agenaises de Gérard de Nerval* (19). Although all of these biographical presentations were certainly of acceptable quality, none gave evidence of the profundity and insight of Léon Cellier's *Gérard de Nerval, l'homme et l'oeuvre* (64), which appeared in 1956 (with a second printing in 1964) and which, like no other critical work of its kind, placed Nerval in a proper literary perspective. Stating his desire to "rejeter quelques idées reçues et quelques préjugés à la mode" (p. 3), Cellier, following a thorough examination of the poet's life, devoted a good part of his book to literary influences, to the literary style and "creation" of the poet, and to Nerval's lofty position in French letters. Furthermore, the last chapter provided a much-needed synthesis of Nerval studies as well as a compendium of "projets à faire." The over-all importance of Professor Cellier's study in the development of Nerval scholarship can hardly be overemphasized.

While the biographers of Nerval were fulfilling their important task, other critics continued to examine closely Gérard's poetic imagery, and especially that in *Les Filles du Feu, Aurélia*, and *Les Chimères*. Raymond Jean, in his 1951 treatment of "Gérard de Nerval et les visages de la nature" (183), touched upon Nerval's Romanticism and the role of nature in *Les Filles du Feu*. Proposing in the same year certain "Notes sur la structure d'*Aurélia*" (69), René Chabrier investigated outstanding symbols in the work and concluded significantly that "[*Aurélia*] échappe partiellement à la critique logique parce que . . . son message fait appel à la toute-puissance d'un principe insaisissable par les méthodes scientifiques, au principe que Platon osait appeler l'AME" (p. 133). The sonnet "El Desdichado" received the attention of Jean Richer, who, in a series of three exhaustive articles (306, 308, 317), attempted to explain the piece in terms of alchemy and the occult sciences. Léon Cellier, who has often justifiably questioned Richer's emphasis, provided an original approach to "El Desdichado" in his article of 1952 entitled "Sur un vers des *Chimères*" (67), in which he viewed the sonnet as the antithetical expression of Nerval's dual personality. Georges Poulet's "Nerval et le cercle onirique" (274) in 1955 was of a more general nature, for it pointed out the image of the clock in *Voyage en Orient, Sylvie, Aurélia,* and Goethe's *Faust* and demonstrated how Nerval attempted to create in the midst of the circular dance of time a single, definable hour, an eternal moment, yet an hour "composée de toutes." In this same area, Egon Huber published a study in 1957 on "Gérard de Nervals Meisternovelle *Sylvie*" (176), in which he showed how multiple themes and images in *Sylvie* are developed in strict accordance with the story's numerical structure.

The résumé above should demonstrate adequately that during the 1950's specialized scholars were interested primarily in the actual details of Nerval's poetic art — symbol, imagery, structure, etc. One meaningful aspect of the poet's work that had been mentioned from time to time but never developed fully was myth and the mythical experience. In 1955 J.-P. Richard included Nerval in his *Poésie et profondeur* (292) and suggested that Gérard's whole poetic creation is built around a mythical quest for personal identity in relation to nature. The following year, Marie-Jeanne Durry received recognition for her treatment of *Gérard de Nerval et le mythe* (121), a work of importance that was to exercise considerable influence on the changing trends in scholarship. Mme Durry maintained that the entire *expérience nervalienne* is portrayed on a mythical level and that the personal myth is created by substituting a collective mental awareness of things for an individual awareness. Furthermore, she noted, by developing partially a personal myth, around which the whole exterior world revolves, Nerval creates an "universalisation du souvenir." Durry's thesis was both plausible and admirable, and it is hardly surprising that Jean Richer's thesis of 1963 (312) treats Nerval's creative process in terms of pre-existing and personal myths.

The year 1955 marked the centenary of Nerval's death, an occasion that was honored by special issues of the *Cahiers du Sud,* the *Mercure de France, Les Nouvelles Littéraires,* and *Le Figaro Littéraire.* Of equal importance was an exposition organized at the Bibliothèque Nationale (252), where 380 items of Nervaliana were placed on display for the public. It is interesting that, from this date on, critical attention was placed not only on major texts but also on more neglected works and subjects. Nerval's role in the

LETTERHEAD FOR A LETTER TO JENNY COLON
LOVENJOUL COLLECTION

NERVAL AT SENLIS

PHOTOGRAPH BY AUTHOR

development of the *chanson populaire*, as well as his talents as a music critic, received complete coverage in Léon Guichard's *La Musique et les lettres au temps du romantisme* (165) of 1955. Three years later Marcel Schneider elaborated on the subject in his "Nerval et la musique" (345), pointing out that, although Gérard demonstrated a remarkable appreciation of great music (being one of the first to recognize the genius of Liszt and Wagner), he was unable to perceive in formalized music the "mystère" that he found in the *chanson populaire*. In 1955 Raymond Jean offered, in his article "Nerval romancier" (185), the most detailed analysis to date of Nerval's one novel, *Le Marquis de Fayolle*, while Jeanne Poirier published the only critical study of the poet's famous *Lettres* to Jenny Colon: "Un Etrange Amoureux: Gérard de Nerval. Autour des lettres à Jenny Colon" (269). Jean Gaulmier's book of 1956, *Gérard de Nerval et les Filles du Feu* (145), was a welcome contribution, for the author both studied in detail *all* of the stories and argued convincingly for the over-all coherence of the collection. Gilbert Rouger's 1950 critical edition of the *Voyage en Orient* stimulated new interest in a work that is considered by many critics the finest, most original example of Romantic travel literature. Louis-A. Christophe devoted four articles (76–79) to certain hitherto neglected aspects of the work, and Hassan El Nouty discussed in his *Le Proche-Orient dans la littérature française de Nerval à Barrès* (173) how, with Nerval's *Voyage en Orient*, travel literature became a specifically defined genre. Since Gérard's Germanism had never been investigated fully, Charles Dédéyan published, between 1957 and 1959, his monumental three-volume study on *Gérard de Nerval et l'Allemagne* (106), which undoubtedly inspired the renewed interest in the topic during the first half of the next decade. In 1957 Jean Richer called attention to the importance of Nerval's theatre in "Le Roman d'un drame: Nerval et *Léo Burckart*" (319) and again, in 1958, in "Nerval et le théâtre" (309), in which he spoke of *Léo Burckart* as "un grand drame romantique injustement méconnu" (p. 12). Yves Le Hir's "La Versification de Gérard de Nerval" (213) of 1956 was the first serious treatment of Gérard's poetic forms, and it was followed two years later by Henri Meschonnic's "Essai sur la poétique de Nerval" (233). Léon Cellier's demand in 1956 (64) for a proper definition of Nerval's Romanticism was met in part by Henri Lemaître's "Gérard deux fois romantique" (214).

Considering Gérard "le plus *complet* — et peut-être le seul vraiment *complet* — de nos romantiques" (p. 9), Lemaître demonstrated the double nature of this writer's Romanticism, which found its expression "entre les mirages du monde extérieur et les mystères du monde intérieur, entre les exaltations de la sensibilité superficielle et les révélations de la sensibilité profonde, entre les fantasmagories de l'imagination et les mythes authentiques de l'âme" (p. 9).

The decade also produced three bibliographical studies. While R.-M. Albérès' "Etat présent des études nervaliennes" (2) of 1955 was a short résumé of only the major critical studies on Nerval up to that year, Léon Cellier, in his commentary "Où en sont les recherches sur Gérard de Nerval?" (65), two years later, proposed a valuable program of research in which "l'oeuvre de Nerval doit être étudiée dans un ordre strictement chronologique, et, selon la méthode de M. Audiat, systématiquement appliquée, ne doit être négligé aucun état du mythe" (p. 13). After discussing the most general trends in Nerval scholarship, Cellier suggested a number of noteworthy topics that he felt should be dealt with more fully: Nerval's theatre, his Romanticism, the influence on his imagination of *Wilhelm Meister* and *Robert le Diable*, "l'univers de Nerval," etc. The paramount importance of Jean Senelier's *Gérard de Nerval: essai de bibliographie* (351) of 1959 is evident in view of the increasing number of books and articles devoted to Nerval during the present decade. The bibliography includes 1,257 listings of primary works and 1,222 secondary items, along with a selection of iconographical documents. Although this work leaves something to be desired in the way of completeness and full documentation of critical references, it is nevertheless the most valuable tool to date for the study of Gérard de Nerval. M. Senelier's *Complément*, to appear in 1968, will be a welcome addition to the 1959 bibliography.

1960–1966

Equipped with the Senelier bibliography, the revised Pléiade edition of 1960 (Vol. I) and 1961 (Vol. II), the first two volumes of the *Oeuvres complémentaires* (which began under Richer's editorship in 1959 and which will include eight volumes of text when completed), and the editor Minard's two series, "Archives Nervaliennes" and "Nouvelle Bibliothèque Nervalienne," scholars of the present decade have encountered few problems related to the availability of texts. As a result, critical interest in Nerval has attained even greater heights during the 1960's and has helped to place Nerval before the general public. As if Proust had forecast the obvious in 1920, Gérard de Nerval is considered now "assurément un des trois ou quatre plus grands écrivains du XIXe siècle."

Although attention is being placed increasingly on Gérard's minor pieces, the four works that have continued to receive most consideration since 1960 are the sonnet "El Desdichado," *Sylvie, Voyage en Orient,* and, above all, *Aurélia.* Shortly before I devoted a Master's thesis to "The Exegesis of Gérard de Nerval's 'El Desdichado'," John Kneller inspired a great deal of interest in the sonnet — both here and abroad — with his commentary of 1960, "The Poet and his Moira: 'El Desdichado'" (197). Unlike those before him (with the clear exception of Albert Béguin), Professor Kneller viewed the poem generally as the revelation of a man's poetical experience, a work of art complete in itself. Acknowledging the possible hermetic sources, but insisting that these sources do not govern the true message of the sonnet, the author suggested a method of approach that was subsequently employed by Albert Gérard and Marie-Thérèse Goosse. Gérard, in his article of 1963 entitled "Images, structure et thèmes dans 'El Desdichado'" (151), studied the poem as an antithetical work of art, containing "une signification perceptible sans références excessives à autre chose que lui-même" (p. 507). Goosse's long explication of 1964, "'El Desdichado' de Gérard de Nerval" (160), adhered generally to the same line of thought but included a full consideration of Nerval's other works and their relationship to "El Desdichado." Jacques Geninasca's more recent *Une Lecture de "El Desdichado"* (149) is the most complete single study of the sonnet to date and will meet undoubtedly with a considerable amount of critical opposition. Jean Pellegrin's "Commentaire sur 'El Desdichado'" (257) strives to show how the poem is a purely artistic statement of a man's desperate search for the absolute, while the short article of Jacques Dhaevens, "A propos de l'établissement du texte de 'El Desdichado,'" (112) points out problems concerning the three manuscripts. It is my opinion that the exegeses of Kneller, Goosse, and especially Gérard are by far the most plausible and will continue to serve as models for future considerations of "El Desdichado" and the other enigmatic sonnets in *Les Chimères.*

Jean Guillaume's critical edition of *Les Chimères* (168) contains a number of new observations on the sonnets, but the book is so poorly organized and so weighed down with superfluous documentation it is virtually unusable.

Alison Fairlie's "An Approach to Nerval" (128) in 1961 demonstrated, perhaps better than any other item, the sophistication of modern Nerval scholarship. While her explications of "El Desdichado" and of "Le Christ aux Oliviers" were sound and absorbingly interesting, the analysis of *Sylvie* was the most important topic of her discussion. Professor Fairlie summed up the results of her reading of *Sylvie* in the following manner: "From both the limpingly natural and the elaborately formalized, Nerval weaves his sense of tenderness, irony, and final persistence" (p. 102). During the same year, Umberto Eco produced one of the most lucid interpretations of "Il Tempo di *Sylvie*" (122), showing how, with Nerval, time gradually begins to define an ultimate tragedy and thus becomes a prelude to death. Ross Chambers dealt in part with the same subject in his "Water in *Sylvie*" (73) of 1963, but he insisted that "underlying the theme of love as well as the theme of time, water serves not only to convey the fundamental unity of these two themes but also to suggest by its own ambivalence that the dualism they imply is an illusory one" (p. 503). The most original critical analysis of *Sylvie* is that included in Raymond Jean's *Nerval par lui-même* (184), in which all aspects of the *nouvelle* are interpreted on various levels.

As a direct result of Dédéyan's *Gérard de Nerval et l'Allemagne* (106), interest in the poet's Germanism has been more obvious than ever. While Marcel Brion's "Gérard de Nerval, romantique allemand" (53) of 1962 placed Nerval "plus près du Romantisme allemand qu'il ne l'était des romantiques français" (p. 22) and traced with some precision the influence of Goethe, Heine, Hoffmann, Jean-Paul, and Novalis, Claude Pichois devoted over ten pages to Gérard de Nerval in his *L'Image de Jean-Paul Richter dans les lettres françaises* (265). The most concentrated study on the subject since the publication of Dédéyan's book is Alfred DuBruck's *Gérard de Nerval and the German Heritage* (113), an interesting and original analysis of the artistic and intellectual relationship between Nerval and Hoffmann, Goethe, and Heine.

It is quite obvious that the major part of Nerval criticism from 1960 to 1967 has been devoted directly or indirectly to *Aurélia*, the work considered by most scholars to be Gérard's masterpiece. In addition to numerous notes and short articles written on the various biographical, stylistic, and mythological aspects of the work, Jean Richer's *Une Collaboration inconnue*: . . . (298) of 1963 and Berthe Reymond's "Le Mythe féminin dans l'oeuvre de Nerval" (284) of the same year seem worthy of special attention. In his 32-page pamphlet, Richer introduced the painter Paul Chenavard, one of Nerval's close friends, whose haunting murals intended for the Panthéon contained much of the same syncretic symbolism as that found in *Aurélia*. After discussing at length the six articles by Gérard and Gautier describing Chenavard's art, Richer concluded that "l'histoire des relations entre Nerval et Chenavard apporte un cas singulier d'influence réciproque de la poésie et de la peinture . . ." (p. 24). Although Berthe Reymond's "Le Mythe féminin dans l'oeuvre de Nerval" was limited to consideration of *Sylvie* and *Aurélia*, her treatment of this important element in the latter work demonstrated generally Nerval's capability of transforming pre-existing myth into personal myth and how, in the poet's best art, unity and multiplicity are counterbalanced to attain equilibrium. Three years later, Georges Poulet developed this idea in an essay on Nerval included in his *Trois Essais de mythologie romantique* (276). In 1965 Jean Richer published a magnificent critical edition of *Aurélia* (295), which includes at the end a series of six articles on the work by three well-known Nervalians. Maria-Luisa Belleli's "*Aurélia* en Italie" (30) and John Kneller's "*Aurélia* across the Channel and the Atlantic" (195) provide adequate summaries of Nerval's (rather than *Aurélia*'s) popularity in Italy, the British Isles, and the United States. In "An Approach to *Aurélia*" (194), Kneller contends that the *expérience* of *Aurélia* should be viewed as a poetic, psychological, and religious experiment, by which the poet creates and elaborates the personal myth. One can hardly praise Belleli's second contribution, "Dramma e linguaggio in *Aurélia*" (31), which, unfortunately, is little more than a superficial attempt to describe Nerval's psychological experience. François Constans' first article, "*Aurélia* ou l'itinéraire de la délivrance" (91), is a rich, comprehensive essay that strives convincingly to define and describe once and for all the artistic unity of *Aurélia*; his second, "Le 'Panorama' de Gérard de Nerval" (96) attempts to decipher and explain the strange allusions in another closely related work.

Critics of the sixties have by no means limited their interests to Nerval's major writings, and they have made efforts to show that Gérard's artistic talents extend into regions other than those of dream and of esoteric literature. Marcel Françon has analyzed in detail Nerval's critical study on the poets of the sixteenth century (133, 134, 137–140) and has tried to establish to what extent the writer was influenced by the Pléiade poets, particularly Ronsard (133). Nerval's role in the development of short fiction has been an increasingly popular topic during the past seven years. Although the subject was considered in Alfred G. Engstrom's "The French Artistic Short Story before Maupassant" (unpublished doctoral dissertation, University of North Carolina, 1941) and was touched upon in two articles by Professor Bandy (13, 14) in 1948 and 1949, Gérard's short stories remained all but forgotten until the present decade. In his *Short Fiction in France, 1800–1850* (150), Albert George recognizes Nerval as a short story writer who went beyond the formal concept of Balzac and Borel and who rejected the rigid form in which Mérimée had encased the short narrative. Michel Glatigny's more recent *"La Main enchantée* de Nerval . . ."* (157) is the most thorough appraisal of what is perhaps Nerval's best story.

In 1960 Robert Montal satisfied partially the pleas of Richer and Cellier for a more thorough investigation of Nerval's theatre. Montal's "Un Curieux Plagiat; *Piquillo* . . ." (238) not only pointed out the highly original qualities of this play but also offered a general commentary on Gérard's theatre and its position in French dramatic tradition. Norma Rinsler's "Nerval, Méry et deux pièces perdues" (332) of 1964 argued convincingly that the two supposedly lost plays of Nerval and Méry (*La Nuit blanche* and *De Paris à Pékin*) are but one and the same. Inspired by Richer's two earlier studies of Nerval's finest drama, *Léo Burckart* (310, 319), Alfred DuBruck has more recently analyzed aspects of the two existing versions of the play in his "Nerval's *Léo Burckart*: Message or Confession" (115), concluding that "the political issues, even though they form the frame of the plot, are and remain of lesser significance" (p. 271). Dennis Sullivan's article of 1965 on "The Function of the Theater in the Work of Nerval" (366) discusses to what extent Gérard was obsessed by a metaphysical concept of the theatre: "Its function is that of a spiritual instrument which is concretely employed [particularly in *Sylvie, Aurélia,* and *Le Prince des Sots*] in [the poet's] quest" (p. 610). According to the author, Nerval's artistic transformation of the world into a theatre allowed him to define the correspondence between the two realms of human experience, giving depth to both the temporal and the eternal mode of existence, to both reality and dream.

The ever-increasing number of books, articles, and notes devoted to diverse aspects of Gérard's life and work demonstrates the scholarly world's interest in and fascination with a poet whose message is of universal value. Many enlightened critical items have appeared since 1960, most of which have treated new and important subjects. While Maria-Luisa Belleli has discussed in two articles (32, 33) the significance of Italy in Nerval's works, André Sempoux (349) and Walter Strauss (364) have emphasized the influence of Dante. Norma Rinsler's study in 1963 of "Classical Literature in the Work of Gérard de Nerval" (323) contends that Nerval's knowledge of classical culture constantly added an extra dimension to both his style and his whole existence. Raymond Jean's "Rousseau selon Nerval" (187) of 1961 and Henri Bonnet's "Poètes de l'adieu: Nerval et Baudelaire" (39) of 1963 are worthy contributions that will surely inspire further considerations in the more comparative areas of research.

The importance of Nerval's journalistic career was touched upon finally in 1960 by Raymond Jean. In his "L'Oeil critique de Gérard de Nerval" (186), Jean stated that to understand fully the poet's use of syncretism, his love of archetypes, and his obsession with the theatre, one must see Nerval as his contemporaries saw him, as "un homme de culture, un merveilleux *liseur*," a man forced by his profession to demonstrate constantly "un oeil critique." S.-O. Simches, in *Le Romantisme et le goût esthétique du XVIIIe siècle* (358) of 1964, emphasized Gérard's attraction to eighteenth-century aesthetic principles, a subject that continues to demand a great deal of critical attention. Norma Rinsler's four articles (324, 327–329) devoted to Nerval's cyclothymic nature have already influenced the research of some scholars and will undoubtedly affect future consideration of the poet's work. In his recent *Gérard de Nerval inconnu* (260), Edouard Peyrouzet has continued the efforts of Béchade-Labarthe (19) to investigate in detail Gérard's background and heredity and to establish some definite relationship between the poet's genealogy and his creative work. Although Peyrouzet's highly original study will meet with some critical opposition, the author is to be praised for shedding further light on a subject that has been unjustifiably neglected.

Most critics would agree that Jean Richer's doctoral thesis of 1963, *Nerval: expérience et création* (312) is, without doubt, the most significant single study to date of Gérard de Nerval. This erudite work is of monumental value and shows the sort of understanding of Nerval that results only from a lifelong devotion. Proposing to "étudier en détail les opérations mentales et les transmutations artistiques qui, au cours d'une existence assez banale quant aux événements extérieurs, permirent à G. Labrunie de devenir . . . ce qu'il voulait être, c'est-à-dire Gérard de Nerval" (p. 11), Richer concentrates strictly on the relationship between Nerval's human experience and his literary creation, including biographical material only when it appears relative and pertinent to the evaluation of the poet's art. The author's coverage of both major and minor works (including such generally neglected pieces as the *Odelettes*, *La Pandora*, and *Le Marquis de Fayolle*), along with his thorough examination of dominant themes, symbols, and myths (for example, the "Napoléonide," "la Race Rouge," and "la Mère et les Mères"), makes this the most scholarly of books published on Nerval.

Raymond Jean's shorter and less specialized study of 1964, *Nerval par lui-même* (184), is intended obviously more for the reading public than for the scholar concerned with the results of advanced research. Jean's objectives are simply to render a faithful portrait of a poet whose name is now well known and to offer a lucid interpretation of the major texts. In his original and well-organized analyses of *Sylvie*, *Aurélia*, and *Les Chimères*, as well as in his probing comments on the close artistic relationship of Proust and Nerval, Raymond Jean demonstrates a rare and possibly unique appreciation of the poet and his work.

Projets à faire

Although the name Gérard de Nerval is now well established in the great hierarchy of French poets, we can by no means consider the critic's task completed. In fact, those who are seriously interested in the advancement of Nerval's literary reputation and in a more perfect appreciation of his art must realize that only the most essential foundation has been laid for a potentially brilliant edifice. We must continue to benefit from the research of such masters as Aristide Marie, Pierre Audiat, Albert Béguin, François Constans, Léon Cellier, and Jean Richer, following their examples in our efforts to attain a richer perspective of the poet and his work. At present we are confronted with an array of critical material on Nerval, much of which will ultimately be discarded as superfluous and virtually insignificant. Additional critical editions will begin to appear, and these new editions will allow Nervalians to view and understand more fully the poet's intricate style, his use of symbol and imagery, and his transformation of artistic elements from one work to another. Senelier's *complément* to the 1959 bibliography will aid considerably the general effort of critics to reinforce our present impressions of Nerval and to place him ultimately on a level with Hugo, Mallarmé, and Baudelaire. I hope this present critical bibliography will play an important role in the future development of Nerval scholarship. Furthermore, we await with eager anticipation the publication of such works as Jean Richer's *Nerval par les témoins de sa vie* and Kurt Schärer's *Thématique de Nerval*, both to be issued by Minard.

Before any well-defined perspective can be acquired on the poet's literary position, certain essential aspects of his work must be investigated more fully. Léon Cellier's demand ten years ago for a proper interpretation of Gérard's "romanticism" has still to be met satisfactorily. It is now generally agreed that Nerval's theatre does not merit extensive consideration, with the exception of *Léo Burckart*. However, the role of the theatre in the poet's life and the importance of his dramatic *feuilletons* are matters that definitely have some bearing on Nerval's creative art and that deserve further consideration. A more attentive reading of Gérard's correspondence (especially the letters addressed to his father and to Dr. Blanche) should reveal a wealth of information on the poet's life and on the composition of his works. The letters to Jenny Colon are not only some of the most beautiful love letters ever written but also they appear to contain the very spiritual essence of the Nervalian *expérience*. Only one critic, Jeanne Poirier (269), has studied the collection in its entirety. While the number of exegeses of "El Desdichado" and "Artémis" seems to multiply each year, less critical attention has been given to the other sonnets that make up *Les Chimères*, all of which ("Le

Christ aux Oliviers" included) demonstrate Nerval's great gifts as a lyric poet. And what of the *Autres Chimères*, which contain the embryo of the poet's mystical vision and which have received appraisal only in Richer's thesis (312)? No significant study has yet been devoted to *Les Illuminés*, an extremely complex work that leads the reader into Nerval's strange esoteric world and that illustrates further the poet's narrative technique. While there are numerous similar topics open to investigation, the one subject that demands immediate attention is Nerval's style, in both his poetry and prose. Except for Henri Meschonnic's purely stylistic analysis (233) of Nerval's sonnet form in 1958 (an article that leaves much to be desired) and Yves le Hir's "La Versification de Gérard de Nerval" of 1956 (213), there has been no important contribution in this area.

Thus, one can assert justifiably that our task has just begun and that we have an obligation not only to those devoted scholars who have endeavored to place the poet in his deserved inheritance, but also to Gérard de Nerval himself. To quote Professor Cellier, "Il y a encore de beaux jours pour les nervaliens."

II. A Critical Bibliography of Nerval Studies from 1900 to 1967

1. Adam, Antoine. "Un Monde plus pur, plus lumineux." *Les Lettres Françaises*, 553 (27 janv.–3 fév. 1955), 1, 5.

As the major precursor of Baudelaire, Rimbaud, and Proust, Nerval tried, more than any other Romantic, to "pousser jusqu'à l'extrème les puissances créatrices de l'esprit." Adam devotes this article to "the other world" of the poet, a world "où tout est calme et beauté, où l'égoïsme, la méchanceté, les passions médiocres n'ont point d'accès," a world so beloved by Marcel Proust.

2. Albérès, R.-M. "Etat présent des études nervaliennes." *Information Littéraire*, VII, no. 5 (1955), 178–85.

A short résumé of only the major critical studies dedicated to Nerval up to the year 1955.

3. ———. *Gérard de Nerval*. Paris: Editions Universitaires, 1955. 126p.

This general but comprehensive study of Nerval demonstrates in the most scholarly fashion a rare understanding and appreciation of the poet. While the author's initial purpose was to analyze the generally neglected tales of *Le Voyage en Orient* and the Octavie-Delfica-Myrtho legend, the study moves into a much broader realm, in which *Sylvie*, *Aurélia*, and *Les Chimères* receive equal consideration. Although the book might be more correctly termed a biography, the admirable method by which Albérès consistently studies and interprets the close relationship between Gérard's life and his poetic creativity enhances the work's critical and highly original value. The author's comments on the difference between Nerval's "vision" and those of Rimbaud and Baudelaire, his interpretation of Nervalian myth and legend, and his view of Gérard's spiritual mysticism are of particular interest. There is a chronological listing of both primary and secondary bibliography at the end of this well-written, well-documented study.
    a. C. Borgal. *Monde Nouveau-Paru*, XI, no. 104 (oct. 1956), 64–70.

4. ———. "Nerval et la rencontre napolitaine." *Figaro Littéraire*, 456 (15 janv. 1955), 4.

Comments on the development of the Octavie-Delfica-Myrtho myth and its relationship with the rite of Isis. The poetic revelation of the "mythe de l'étrangère" can be considered in terms of the following progression: 1834, the

actual encounter with Octavie, possibly at Naples; 1841, the realistic anecdote
of the episode as related in *Les Amours de Vienne*; 1842–43, the poetic treatment of the encounter in *Octavie* and the sonnet "Delfica"; 1845, the mystical
transmutation of the adventure in *Isis*; and 1854, the affirmation of the accom-
plished rite in the sonnet "Myrtho."

5. ———. "Pour rejoindre son rêve éveillé." *Figaro Littéraire*, 456 (15 janv.
    1955), 1.

A short commentary on "la légende" created by Nerval.

6. Antoine, Gérald. "Pour une méthode d'analyse stylistique des images," in
    Langue et littérature (Actes du VIIIe Congrès et Colloques de l'Université de
    Liège, 21). Paris: Les Belles Lettres, 1961.

Discusses the difference in spiritual concept of the "soleil noir" as it appears
in Nerval's "El Desdichado," in Hugo's *La Légende des siècles* ("Inféri"),
and in Baudelaire's *Petits Poèmes en prose* ("Le Désir de peindre"). Whereas
Nerval " 'porte' le soleil noir d'une abstraction, ce qui fait de son image un
emblème et de son Prince une effigie allégorique," Hugo "sees" the image as
a vision and Baudelaire interprets it as one living aspect of the human soul.
The best stylistic study of the image.

7. Audiat, Pierre. *L'Aurélia de Gérard de Nerval*. Paris: Librairie Ancienne
    Honoré Champion, 1926. 131p.

In this admirable thesis devoted to Nerval's masterpiece, the author demonstrates chronologically how each of the poet's works represents a state, an
element, or a stage in the gradual development of a single, personal myth.
Audiat does not attempt to analyze the various elements of *Aurélia*, nor does
he try to indicate any immediate origins of the work. "Il nous suffit," he ex-
plains, "d'avoir essayé d'en retracer la 'biographie,' de l'avoir accompagnée
vivant dans la pensée de Gérard jusqu'au moment où elle va s'exprimer et
. . . mourir" (p. 124). While considerable attention is given in Chapter I to
"La Composition d'*Aurélia*," Chapter II, "Les Documents," brings together all
authentic materials and documents relating to actual or mythical aspects of
the work. The author expresses the hope that in the third chapter, "Les Etats
successifs d'*Aurélia*," "il sera facile de voir comment Gérard . . . a utilisé
littérairement [les documents], comment il les a transformés, déformés et
comment *Aurélia* n'est que le dernier état d'une oeuvre qui a revêtu successivement plusieurs formes" (p. 28).
    a. P. Martino. *Revue Critique d'Histoire et de Littérature* (1927), 449–50.

8. Aunos y Perez, Eduardo. *Gérard de Nerval et ses énigmes*. Paris: Gérard
    Vidal, 1956. 97p.

An original, well-organized approach to many significant facets of Nerval's
life and his poetic work. The author studies initially the dominating image
of the lost mother as the major element of the Nervalian enigma ("Cette
tragédie intime transparaît dans toutes ses oeuvres, leur communiquant un
sentiment d'incertitude" [pp. 19–20]), as well as the profound influence of
Francesco Colonna's *Le Songe de Polyphile* on the poet's creation of his
"amour idéal," his "rêve d'amour," and his constant effort to reconcile earthly
with spiritual love. While Chapter III emphasizes the role of music in Nerval's
amorous and poetic experience, the following chapter dwells on the alchemical

figure of Pandora, ". . . l'image de l'amour total dans lequel coexistent la possibilité de la chute et l'espoir du salut, conjugués selon la réalité intime de ce sentiment" (p. 49). An interesting analysis of the "régéneration mystagogue" of *Aurélia* is reinforced convincingly in a concluding chapter on myth and symbol and in the poet's "descente aux enfers," which is interpreted in three phases: fallen Adam, man's inclination toward the divinity and the faith in his ancestors, and the final confession.

9. Auriant. "Autour de Gérard de Nerval, de William Lane et Makrisi." *Revue de Littérature Comparée*, XXV (1951), 101–26.

Discusses the relationship between Nerval and Edward William Lane and to what extent the latter's *An Account of the Manners and Customs of the Modern Egyptians* influenced Gérard's trip to the Orient and his descriptions in *Le Voyage en Orient*. As Auriant sees it, "Lane lui ouvrit toutes les portes, même les plus secrètes, non avec une clé en bois, mais avec une clé magique."

10. ———. "Deux aspects inconnus de Gérard de Nerval." *Le Bayou*, XII, no. 64 (1955), 473–91.

One of the most informative commentaries on Nerval's career as a journalist and on his political convictions and activity. With regard to Gérard's dramatic criticism published in *L'Artiste*, Auriant very aptly supports his belief that "Dans ces feuillets . . . il s'était livré tout entier, sans détours ni reticences, sans retouches comme sans feintes, avec ses goûts et ses dégoûts, ses admirations et ses haines. . . ." He relates the circumstances behind the poet's dramatic productivity and demonstrates how certain elements in such plays as *Léo Burckart, Les Monténégrins, De Paris à Pékin,* and *Charriot d'argent* represent Gérard's true nature and aspirations.

11. Balakian, Anna. *Literary Origins of Surrealism*. New York: King's Crown Press, 1947. 159p.

With emphasis on the time element as projected in *Aurélia*, the critic examines on pp. 31–44 the various aspects of the poet's masterpiece, which exercised influence on the development of both Symbolist and Surrealist doctrines. She discusses at some length Nerval's distortion of perspective, stating that "this type of exteriorization will contribute considerable significance to the general distortion of perspective which will be attempted by the seekers of surreality" (p. 36).

12. Baldensperger, Fernand. "Gérard de Nerval en Egypte." *L'Alsace Française*, XXVI (oct. 1933), 737–39.

A brief résumé of Nerval's *Voyage en Orient*. The article was inspired by Pierre Martino's presentation of "Le 'Carnet' du *Voyage en Orient*," in *RLC*, no. 1 (janv.–mars 1933), 140–73, and by Jean-Marie Carré's *Voyageurs et écrivains français en Egypte* of 1932.

13. Bandy, W. T. "A propos des plagiats présumés de Gérard de Nerval." *Revue de Littérature Comparée*, XXIII (1949), 94–96.

Offers convincing proof that the short story *La Sonate du Diable* is not by Nerval and therefore should not be included amongst the *Nouvelles et Fantaisies*.

14. ———. "Deux plagiats inconnus de Gérard de Nerval." *Revue de Littérature Comparée*, XXII (1948), 408–15.

Commenting on Marsan's 1928 edition of the *Nouvelles et Fantaisies*, the author points out two *contes* (*La Métempsychose* and *Le Barbier de Goëttingue*) that are definitely not by Nerval, and two others (*La Sonate du Diable* and *Le Portrait du Diable*) that he feels should not be included among the poet's works. Both *La Métempsychose* and *Le Barbier de Goëttingue* are merely translations of Robert Macnish's English articles with the same titles which appeared in *Blackwood's Magazine* in 1826. Nerval not only translated the articles, but he also translated Macnish's signature, "A Modern Pythagorean."

15. ———. "Nervaliana: Gérard's 'Duel' with Dumas; A Forgotten Anecdote." *Studi Francesi*, VII (1963), 473–74.

First reproduces from the review *La Manche* a variant version of an amusing letter by Nerval describing a clever tactic of Alexandre Dumas, and second reproduces an anecdote entitled "Le Chat de Gérard," which appeared in *Le Corsaire-Satan* in 1845 and which was possibly written by Baudelaire.

16. Bassan, Fernande. "Chateaubriand, Lamartine, Nerval, and Flaubert in Palestine." *University of Toronto Quarterly*, XXXIII, no. 2 (1964), 142–63.

A short résumé of Gerard's and his companion Joseph de Fonfrède's trip to the East in 1842 is followed by opinions as to the later influence of this trip on the poet. The critic believes that of all the travel books on the Levant written by Europeans during the first half of the nineteenth century, Nerval's *Voyage en Orient* is the only one that remains interesting and can still be read with pleasure. He concludes that "Nerval's trip revealed to him the presence within him of a strange and mysterious sensitivity which he thought would enable him to penetrate into the innermost secrets of human destiny."

17. Baudouin, Charles. "Gérard de Nerval ou le nouvel Orphée." *Psyché*, I–II, no. 3 (1947), 8–14.

Distinguishes Nerval as one of the first French folklorists and points out the poet's hitherto unnoticed version of the old folk tune "Filles de la Rochelle, Jean Renaud, Le duc Lays est sur un pont, Dessous le rosier blanc. . . ." The author notes that Gérard's version is distinguished by "une sobriété, un juste choix du trait essentiel, qui laissent penser que Nerval a été, ici, un peu plus qu'un scribe." He also touches on other subjects such as Nerval's Orphic role, the eternal Feminine and *la Mère*, and the *double* motif (interpreted in terms of the Jungian *ombre* and the *anima* of *Aurélia*).

18. Bays, Gwendolyn. *The Orphic Vision: Seer Poets from Novalis to Rimbaud*. Lincoln: University of Nebraska Press, 1964. 303p.

In the chapter entitled "The Seer Poet as Syncretist and Interpreter of Myth" (pp. 88–96), the author demonstrates how Nerval projected the visionary powers that were to influence Baudelaire and Rimbaud. She notes that "second sight in the Nervalian sense means the ability to see and to decipher the spiritual significance of events" (p. 89), and that the basis for these powers is created and developed from the poet's knowledge of the occult sciences. Further comments on the occult in literary creation are included in an analysis of the legends of Kalif Hakem and Adoniram and of the symbolism in the *Chimères*, identified as "the jewels of the alchemist in search of perfection" (p. 96).

19. Béchade-Labarthe, Jean. *Origines agenaises de Gérard de Nerval*. Agen: Yves Dubois, 1956. 32p.

In this short study, the author points out the neglected importance of Nerval's Agenais background, which, he feels, influenced the poet as much or more than did his Valois heritage. In this southern region where his father was born, Gérard listened to the Gascon folk tunes and absorbed the folklore of the Poitou area. In the light of such influence on the poet, Béchade-Labarthe explicates the sonnet "El Desdichado," concluding that "Le Prince d'Aquitaine, Phébus, Lusignan, Biron, une sirène, une fée nous ramènent au pays paternel de Gérard," and that all of these personages demonstrate "un passé terrible et fatal de faute, de disgrâce, de refus, de pardon dans une chute irrémédiable." (cf. 260)

    a. A. Got. *Les Lettres Françaises*, no. 656 (6 fév. 1957), 1, 7.

20. Becker, Raymond de. "*Aurélia*, notes psychologiques." *Tour Saint-Jacques*, 13–14 (1958), 65–73.

A convincing interpretation of Nerval's dream world and the nature of the poet's "intuition de la mort." Unlike Dante, Nerval failed in his attempt to sublimate his own being in favor of a spiritual ideal; Aurélia's death signified only that which was dead in the poet. At the end of *Aurélia* Gérard felt he was saved; but "sa mort demeure un démenti de la nature aux illusions que ses derniers moments purent créer." The author establishes four related themes in *Aurélia* that demonstrate the poet's failure: "le soleil couchant," "la descente d'escaliers," "le vieillard inconnu," and "le double."

21. Beguin, Albert. *L'Ame romantique et le rêve*. Paris: José Corti, 1939 [1960]. 416p.

In this monumental essay on the influence of German romanticism on French poetry, Béguin analyzes (in the chapter entitled "Naissance de la poésie: Gérard de Nerval," pp. 358–66) the role that dream plays in Nerval's transfiguration of reality into personal myth. He examines the various stages of "le rêve" in *Aurélia* and concludes that it was in this realm that Gérard found "un moyen de découverte: non seulement de découverte de soi-même, mais de connaissance de l'ultime réalité" (p. 365).

22. ———. *Gérard de Nerval*. Paris: José Corti, 1945. 136p. ["Les Poésies de Gérard de Nerval," pp. 97–105, first printed as "La Poésie de Nerval," in *Les Lettres Françaises*, LXIX (18 août 1945), 3; "Gérard de Nerval et sa Descente aux Enfers," pp. 7–69, first printed in *Gérard de Nerval, suivi de Poésie et Mystique*. Paris: Stock, 1936, pp. 11–96.]

This study, which demonstrates a very sensitive understanding and appreciation of the poet, continues to be respected as one of the most erudite treatments of Nerval's poetry, *Les Filles du Feu*, and, in particular, *Aurélia*. In the first and last chapters, both devoted to *Aurélia*, the author sees Gérard as the hero, who, in his attempt to gain "la lumière suprême," relates "l'histoire d'une lutte titanique, quis'achève par un triomphe" (p. 9). In this poetic revelation of one man's destiny, controlled by the dominating image of "la Femme maternelle," there is no trace of incoherence. Béguin points out the three spiritual levels on which the *récit* is constructed, levels that ultimately blend to create "le drame de la connaissance" and that allow the poet to transcend, by means of love and charity, "l'insoutenable existence du mal" (pp. 129–30). In the chapter "Les Poésies de Nerval," the author depicts the image of the "exilé," always in search of "l'autre patrie, le Pays sans nom" (p. 97). With keen insight, he differentiates and comments on the three ages of the poet, represented by the early nationalistic poems, the *Odelettes*, and the *Chimères*.

    a. X. Tillette. *Etudes* (1946), 286–87.

    b. L. Daudet. *Candide* (18 mars 1957).

23. ———. *Gérard de Nerval et sa Descente aux Enfers.* Paris: Stock, 1937.

See 22.

24. ———. *Gérard de Nerval, suivi de Poésie et Mystique.* Paris: Stock, 1936. 144p.

See 22.

25. ———. "Nerval." *L'Eternelle Revue*, no. 4 (1947), 24–30.

See 22: "Aurélia dans l'oeuvre de Nerval," pp. 125–36.

26. ———. "Nerval en 1949." *Cahiers du Sud*, XXVIII, no. 292 (1948), 393–96.

As the title would suggest, this note is not an "état présent" and represents an acknowledgment and appreciation not merely of a hero but of a man "[qui] demeure aussi modestement invisible dans le désastre que dans le bonheur."

27. ———. *Poésie de la Présence: De Chrétien de Troyes à Pierre Emmanuel.* Neuchâtel: La Baconnière; Paris: Editions du Seuil, 1957. 362p.

Includes general comments on the poetry of the *Chimères* and concludes: "La magie du poème reste aussi mystérieuse après [les] commentaires qu'avant; c'est qu'ils n'*expliquent* rien. Ce qui compte, ce n'est pas le sens littéral, analysable, qui se cache sous les mots et se perçoit par leur musique autant que par leur signification" (pp. 141–42).

    a. *Revue d'Histoire Littéraire de la France*, LXIII, no. 1 (1963), 142–43.

28. ———. "La Poésie de Nerval." *Les Lettres Françaises*, LXIX (18 août 1945), 3.

See 22.

29. ———. "Le Songe de Jean-Paul et Victor Hugo." *Revue de Littérature Comparée*, XIV (1934), 703–13.

A fascinating commentary on the literary influence of Jean-Paul on Hugo and Nerval. Although the major part of the article concentrates on Hugo's use of Jean-Paulian imagery in such poems as "La Chauve-Souris" and "Ce que dit la Bouche d'Ombre," Béguin, suggesting that Hugo more than likely drew from the *Chimères* in his development of the "soleil noir" and the "oeil de Dieu," offers a parallel analysis of "Le Christ aux Oliviers" and certain of Hugo's mystical poems. (cf. 265)

30. Belleli, Maria-Luisa. *"Aurélia* en Italie," in *Aurélia ou le rêve et la vie* (édition critique de Jean Richer). Paris: Minard, 1965, pp. 329–33.

Noting that Nerval is known in Italy by specialists in French literature but not by the general public, the author points out the names of the major Italian critics who have recognized the importance of the poet. A section on "Jugements italiens sur *Aurélia"* is followed by a short bibliography of Italian editions and studies on Nerval.

31. ――――. "Dramma e linguaggio in *Aurélia,"* in *Aurélia ou le rêve et la vie* (édition critique de Jean Richer). Paris: Minard, 1965, pp. 299–325. [Résumé in French, pp. 326–28.]

A very superficial description of the poetic and psychological experience ("Dramma") in *Aurélia*. The reader is weighed down by a vast number of generalities, only to realize at the end that the author has said very little and offered few original ideas. Her final comments on Dante's and Tasso's influence on Nerval are mere repetitions of the opinions expressed in 32 and 33.

32. ――――. "L'Italie de Nerval." *Revue de Littérature Comparée*, XXXIV (1960), 378–408.

The most important general study on the influence of Italy on Nerval's life and work. Gérard loved Italy for reasons exactly the opposite of those that drew him toward Germany. Transforming all of reality into the personal myth, the poet found, in the art and literature of Italy as well as in the Italian countryside, a certain rapport with his own life and his spiritual aspirations. Whether it was in the mysticism of Dante, in Renaissance Neo-Platonism, in the image of Woman as portrayed in Italian paintings, or in the mysterious Pausilippo, Gérard's attraction to Italy and Italian things brought on a nostalgia that was to affect always his poetic view of life. Belleli discusses in relative detail the image of Caravaggio's "Judith," Francesco Colonna's *Songe de Polyphile*, the concept of "Bionda e Grassota," the city of Naples, and Dante. The author feels that although Gérard came under the direct inspiration of the Italian poet's philosophic concept of pure love, "Nerval semble ne pas faire de distinction entre la *Vita Nuova* et la *Divine Comédie"*; he fused the two works into a single and more personal concept.

  a. A. Sempoux. "Nerval et Dante," *Revue de Littérature Comparée*, XXXV (1961), 254–58.

33. ――――. "Note sur Nerval et le Tasse." *Revue des Sciences Humaines*, Fasc. 111 (1963), 371–82.

Although Nerval was without doubt familiar with all of Tasso's *Jerusalem Delivered*, he was probably impressed primarily by the nineteen stanzas of the epic that relate the vision to which he is referring in the "Dédicace à Dumas" when he mentions "la vision du Tasse." Belleli suggests numerous parallels between Nerval and Tasso and recalls the fact that Tasso had spent a great deal of time in Gérard's native Valois country. The Italian poet's communications with exalted spirits, his love for Leonora d'Este, his projection of the dream world into reality all appear to be reflected in *Aurélia* and other works by Nerval. Belleli suggests finally that Gérard was perhaps the only one of the French Romantics who was interested in the Neo-Platonic elements in Tasso's work.

34. ———. "Il Volto giovanile di Nerval." *La Fiera Letteraria*, XV (6 marzo 1960), 4.

While commenting on the pillar erected in honor of Nerval at the Tour Saint-Jacques, the author makes an interesting comparison between the poet's youthful poetry and the later *Chimères*, which "proclamano, in una forma perfetta, verità a volte oscure di un sognato sincretismo religioso, con una forza che viene tutta dal bisogno sentimentale e spirituale di comporre dei miti."

35. Bérence, Fred. "Fils de Cain." *Nouvelles Littéraires* (29 mai 1958), 5. [Reprinted as "Nerval; fils du Cain" in *Grandeur spirituelle du XIXe siècle*. Vol. II. Paris, 1959, pp. 90–110.]

A biographical résumé. The title refers to Hiram, a descendant of Cain. "Nerval se veut frère d'Hiram."

36. ———. *Grandeur spirituelle du XIXe siècle*. Paris, 1959. 2 vols.
See 33.

37. Billy, André. "L'Erudition de Nerval et celle d'Apollinaire." *Figaro Littéraire* (5 fév. 1955), 5.

A brief commentary on Nerval and his influence on Apollinaire and Fernand Fleuret.

38. Bizet, René. *La Double Vie de Gérard de Nerval*. Paris: Librairie Plon, 1928. 255p.

In this biography of Nerval, the author attempts to reconcile the poet's dream world with the world of reality. Although Bizet restricts himself to *Sylvie* and *Aurélia* in his very personal discussion of Nerval's life, the emphasis he places on the "poet of Paris," Jenny Colon, and the *Second Faust* leads to some interesting observations on Gérard's double existence.

39. Bonnet, Henri. "Poètes de l'adieu: Nerval et Baudelaire." *Les Humanités*, 386 (mai 1963), 17–25.

Pages 17–21 are devoted to a lucid *explication de texte* of Chapter IX of *Sylvie*. Attentive analysis of the passage results in the following conclusion: *Sylvie* is "le poème du souvenir et de l'adieu. . . . Il apparaît bien que les deux sentiments sont mêlés: le souvenir d'un bonheur 'aboli' ne peut que donner une coloration sombre à un paysage aimé et recréer douloureusement l'enchantement du passé." At the end of the essay, an interesting parallel is drawn between Nerval's passage and Baudelaire's "Chant d'Automne."

40. Borel, Pierre. "*Sylvie, Aurélia* et le 'carnet rose' de Gérard de Nerval." *Une Semaine dans le Monde* (19 avril 1947), 11.

A short commentary of little value on the recovered "petit carnet rose saumon," which, according to the author, Nerval completed in 1840, carried with him on his travels, and later expanded into his masterpiece *Aurélia*.

41. Borgal, Clément. *De quoi vivait Gérard de Nerval.* Paris: Les Deux Rives, 1950 ("De quoi vivaient-ils?" no. 5). 127p.

Discusses briefly the various means by which Nerval tempted Fate and tried to comprehend his illness. Main emphasis is on biography. Of very little scholarly value.

42. ———. "Gérard de Nerval ou la passion du jeu." *Monde Nouveau-Paru*, XI, no. 104 (1956), 64–70.

Sees in the background of Nerval's poetic originality his "passion du jeu," his ability to always undertake a role, which he played "avec son esprit et son imagination." Nerval found his other existence in "le jeu": "Il n'a pas fallu moins d'une existence pour connaître qu'il y a du sacré dans le jeu, comme il entre une part de jeu dans la religion."

43. Bosquet, Alain. *Verbe et vertige. Situation de la poésie.* Paris: Hachette, 1961. 373p.

In this rather interesting study on poetic form, the author discusses Nerval, along with Baudelaire, as the poet who introduced in his verse a new and modern concept: that poetry must be more than "écriture"; it must be "langage," and it must "signifier" that which no other language can demonstrate. Thus, with Gérard de Nerval, "[la poésie] constitue une origine, à partir de laquelle il est possible d'élaborer soit un panorama de sensations, soit une échelle de valeurs imaginaires. Elle n'est pas le résultat calculé, de rien que l'on puisse définir avec précision, mais elle est bien le tremplin qui va servir aux esprits étonnés à plonger dans un vaste bassin d'intentions gauchies d'images à multiples sens, de significations tronquées et à la fois délirantes" (p. 40).
    a. Maria L. A. Marenzi. *Annali della Facoltà di Lingue e Letterature Straniere di ca'Foscari*, II (1963), 169–72.

44. Bosquet, Jacques. *Les Thèmes du rêve dans la littérature romantique (France, Angleterre, Allemagne).* Paris: Didier, 1964 ("Etudes de Littérature Etrangère et Comparée," 47). 656p.

Since the primary purpose of this monumental study is to "déterminer aussi rigoureusement que possible comment naissent, vivent et meurent, les images oniriques" (p. 9), the reader will not find a literary interpretation of Nerval's artistic expression of the dream. Instead, the author methodically refers to Nerval throughout the study as a significant writer of "dream literature" and simply points out representative oneiric states as they appear in the poet's works, particularly in *Aurélia*.

45. Boucoiran, Jean. *La Sylvie de Gérard de Nerval.* Nimes: Lapeyre-Tallez, 1933. 103p.

One of the earliest and most stimulating attempts to analyze *Sylvie* as a work of art. Although most of the critical observations in the six chapters concern the *nouvelle* (and to some extent, *Les Filles du Feu* in general), the second chapter, "Illuminisme et germanisme" (pp. 29–42), anticipates later emphasis on the poet's esoteric nature.
    a. D. Mornet. *Revue d'Histoire Littéraire de la France* (juillet-sept. 1934), 460–61.

46. Boulanger, Jacques. *Au Pays de Gérard de Nerval.* Paris: Honoré Champion, 1914. 207p.

Discusses the historical development of such towns in the Valois as Loisy, Mortefontaine, Châalis, Ermenonville, and Senlis and their significance in *Les Filles du Feu.* Well documented.

47. Bounoure, Gabriel. "La Rose de Choubrah." *Lettres Nouvelles,* LXII (1958), 444–49.

Interprets this image from *Aurélia* in terms of Tarot Card No. 17. The Rose of Choubrah was for Gérard a means of composing "l'homme total," a model for which he was constantly searching and which was made up of "l'unité dans la diversité." Whether it is a question of this or any other rose, or any image, the "étoile," the "reine," the "fée," the "citron," etc., Nerval composes his great poem of words that are "les 'vocables-clefs' qui déclenchent une circulation entre réel et imaginaire."

48. ———. "Sophianité de Gérard." *La Tour Saint-Jacques,* 13–14 (1958), 91–99.

An important commentary on Nerval's "Féminin céleste," which is composed of "la Consolatrice, la Soeur, la Mère, l'Amante, Celle qui donne la vie," and unified in the theopanic figure of Sophia (Sophie), "la Reine du Matin," the divine Ideal who guides the poet out of the darkness of death into the light of spiritual reintegration. Gérard tried to dissolve the universal "double" and restore the lost "Soi" to itself by creating the androgynous Sophia, "la fusion d'Adam, l'Homme Rouge, avec la blancheur de l'essence féminine." Balkis and Sett El Moulk, both sister and wife of Adoniram and Hakim, best represent this aspect of the poet's desire and imagination: ". . . l'union avec la soeur consolide l'identité du héros. . . . Seule une union avec une créature du même sang, avec la Soeur, avec le Double féminin permettra à Hakim de rejoindre son âme à l'âme du monde et d'entrer dans la vie divine." In this same light, the critic discusses the figures of Adrienne, Sylvie, Pandora, the Queen of Sheba, and Artémis.

49. Bourin, André. "Les Itinéraires familiers de Gérard de Nerval: Paris; Le Valois." *Nouvelles Littéraires* (29 mai 1958), 6–7.

Retraces with some precision the areas of Paris and of the Valois country as described by Nerval in his works. The author attempts to describe exactly what these geographical locations meant to the poet and their importance in Nerval's art.

50. ———. "Les Trois Morts de Nerval." *Nouvelles Littéraires* (29 mai 1958), 5.

Presents the three major interpretations of Gérard's suicide: those of Jean Richer ("le suicide mystique"), Jean Pommier ("le suicide d'imitation, d'après celui du dernier des Condé"), and Pierre Audiat ("le suicide dans un moment de dépression anxieuse").

51. Bremond, Henri. *La Poésie pure.* Paris: Bernard Grasset, 1926. 321p.

Although the author includes "El Desdichado" as an example of "pure poetry" (see pp. 15–27), the relationship established between the evocative power of Nerval's verse and that of the later Symbolist poetry appears quite distorted.

52. Breuillac, Marcel. "Hoffmann en France." *Revue d'Histoire Littéraire de la France*, XIV (1907), 74–105.

In this three-part study of Hoffmann's early literary vogue in France, the author devotes considerable attention to the rapport between Nerval's work and that of the German master. It is suggested that Gérard was attracted to Hoffmann not merely for literary reasons but even more because he admired the erratic nature of this poet of the bizarre and fantastic.

53. Brion, Marcel. "Gérard de Nerval, romantique allemand." *Revue de Paris*, LXIX, no. 8 (1962), 15–27.

One of the most lucid considerations of Nerval's Germanism. Convinced that Gérard was "plus près du Romantisme allemand qu'il ne l'était des romantiques français," the author traces the influence on Nerval of Goethe, Heine, Hoffmann, Jean-Paul, and Novalis. He notes that while Nerval most admired in Hoffmann the theme of the "double" ("doppelgänger"), he discovered in Jean-Paul the means by which to carry out his "épanouissement du rêve." The possible influence of Novalis' *Les Disciples à Saïs* is also suggested.
   a. R. Ciureanu. *Studi Francesi*, XVIII (1962), 573.

54. Carco, Francis. *Gérard de Nerval*. Paris: Albin Michel, 1953. 160p.

A short undocumented biography that demonstrates a sincere appreciation of the poet but offers few original ideas.
   a. J. Follain. *La Table Ronde*, LXX (oct. 1953), 132.

55. Cargo, Robert T. "Gérard de Nerval's Benoni." *Romance Notes*, VII, no. 1 (1965), 12–15.

Like DuBruck (114), the author points out the name Benoni (Adoniram's companion in *Voyage en Orient*) in Genesis 35:18. Supplementary suggestions as to probable reasons for Nerval's choice of this particular biblical name are important and demonstrate further the poet's linguistic and cultural-religious interests.

56. Carré, Jean-Marie. *Voyageurs et écrivains français en Egypte, II*. Le Caire: Institut Français d'Archéologie Orientale, 1932. 400p.

Chapter I (pp. 1–45) includes an exceptionally fine commentary on the art and composition of the *Voyage en Orient*, considered here to be perhaps Nerval's most imaginative work. Stating that "il y a, dans son récit, plus de poésie que de vérité" (p. 17), Carré studies attentively the carefully planned architecture of the work and notes how Gérard went so far as to remove all dates in order to reinforce continuity and over-all structure. The *Voyage en Orient* is not a journal but an artistically developed *récit*, composed after Nerval's return to France and based on his notes and memories of the trip. If the poet distorts reality, "ce n'est pas . . . pour se faire valoir, mais pour la faire revivre plus complètement, lui conférer le prestige et la durée des créations éternelles de l'art" (p. 17). The second part of the discussion concerns Nerval's actual trip and points out such interesting facts as the poet's inability to speak Arabic.
   a. P. Martino. *Revue de Littérature Comparée* (juillet-sept. 1934).

57. Carrouges, Michel. "Les Pouvoirs de la femme selon Nerval et Breton."
    Cahiers du Sud, XXVIII, no. 292 (1948), 419–29.

Throughout Nerval's work reverberates the cry of Mélusine and the overwhelming power she exerts over the poet. In *Aurélia* we see the supreme concept of "la Femme," in whose hand "tous les pouvoirs du ciel avec ceux de la
terre sont réunis." The poet calls her the eternal Isis (the Great Mother and
holy spouse), the ancient Venus, and the Holy Virgin of the Christians. With
Nerval she evolves into a totally religious being, a conciliator between man
and nature. She is herself "reconciliation," "le foyer vivant où rayonnent en
tous sens les fleuves de la vie."

58. Cartier, Julia. *Un Intermédiaire entre la France et l'Allemagne: Gérard de
    Nerval.* Genève: Société Générale d'Imprimerie, 1904. 130p.

The first academic thesis devoted to Gérard de Nerval and the first serious
treatment of the poet's debt to German literature. This pioneer study, based
on the Michel Lévy edition of Nerval's works and on a certain number of unpublished texts, emphasizes Nerval's role as the translator of German authors and
as the Romantic traveler. One notes at this early date such interesting critical
opinions as "C'est à peine si l'on peut dire que l'Allemagne a révélé Gérard de
Nerval à lui-même" (p. 115). The author arrives at the general conclusion that
Gérard's direct borrowings from German literature resulted in such inferior
works as *L'Imagier de Harlem* and *La Misanthropie* and that Germany served
only to awaken in the poet his interest in folk-songs.

59. Castelli, Fernando. "Gérard de Nerval." *Letture*, XV, no. 10 (1960), 643–52.

Stating that he wishes "sopratutto soffermarci a cogliere l'amima dell'avventura
nervaliana per poter captare quel significato in sé," Castelli distinguishes what
he considers the four major elements to be studied in Nerval's work: occultism,
religious syncretism, magnetism, and Romanticism. Devoting special attention
to *Aurélia* and the poet's religious problem, the author disagrees with Béguin's
contention (22) that Gérard describes a basically Christian experience at the
end of the *récit*: ". . . Nerval per il cristianesimo ha avuto solo momenti sin-
ceri e vibranti di nostalgia, presto assorbiti nell'arruffio del suo sincretismo.
Null'altro. Non ci si può affidare ad alcune frasi, sia pur significativi, d'uno
spirito così fluido e cangiante." A bibliography and a valuable list of Italian
translations of Nerval's works are included in the middle of the article.
    a. G. Franceschetti. *Studi Francesi*, XVI (1962), 172.

60. ———. *Letterature dell'inquietudine* (Baudelaire, Nerval, Rimbaud, etc.).
    Milano: Massimo, 1963. 549p.

Contains the opinions of 59.
    a. F. Casnati. *L'Osservatore Romano*, 19–20 (agosto 1963), 3.

61. Castex, Pierre-George. *Le Conte fantastique en France de Nodier à Maupas-
    sant.* Paris: José Corti, 1951. 466p.

Includes commentary on Nerval's role in the development of French short
prose fiction and, more specifically, on his indebtedness to Hoffmann. Gérard
was attracted to Hoffmann's subject matter as a result of his own personal
drama, which allowed him to transform and develop in a new genre much of

the German writer's romanesque material. Most readers will agree that Castex
leans a little too heavily on Sébillotte's psychological analysis of Nerval and,
at times, loses sight of the poet's very natural, Romantic inclination toward
the fantastic tale.

62. Cattaui, Georges. *Orphisme et prophétie chez les poètes français: 1850–1959*
(Hugo, Nerval, Baudelaire, Rimbaud, Mallarmé, Claudel, Valéry). Paris:
Plon, 1965.

Pages 60–81 discuss Nerval as an Orphic poet and demonstrate the Orphic
elements in his major work.

63. Cavé, Madelaine, et Gisèle Marie. "Gérard aima-t-il Jenny Colon ou la comtesse d'Egmont?" *Nouvelles Littéraires* (29 mai 1958), 1, 10.

See 223.

64. Cellier, Léon. *Gérard de Nerval, l'homme et l'oeuvre*. Paris: Hatier, 1956.
255p. ["Connaissance des Lettres," 48.]

One of the finest, most lucid studies of Gérard de Nerval. Professor Cellier,
benefiting from the research of other distinguished Nerval scholars, attempts
to "rejeter quelques idées reçues et quelques préjugés à la mode" and to place
Nerval in his proper literary perspective. After a thorough examination of the
poet's life (5 chapters), Cellier devotes the remainder of his book to literary
influences, to the literary style and "création" of the poet ("Une Ame romantique" and "Le Créateur"), and to Nerval's lofty position in French letters.
The last chapter, entitled "La Montée lumineuse," provides an admirable
synthesis of modern Nerval studies as well as a compendium of "projets à
faire." A "Note bibliographique" points out major editions and critical studies
of the poet and his work.
    a. A. G. Engstrom. *Modern Language Notes*, LXXIII (1958), 139–43.
    b. R. Lacoste. *Lettres Françaises*, no. 658 (14–20 fév. 1957), 3.
    c. C. Pichois. *Revue d'Histoire Littéraire de la France*, LVIII (juillet–sept.
       1958), 404–6.
    d. J. H. Thomas. *French Studies*, XII (1958), 381.
    e. P. Vincensini. *Revue de Littérature Comparée*, XXXVIII, no. 4 (1964),
       614–17.

65. ———. *Où en sont les recherches sur Gérard de Nerval?* Paris: Minard, 1957.
32p. [Archives des Lettres Modernes; Archives Nervaliennes, 2.]

While the main purpose of this superb study is to "proposer un programme
de recherches," M. Cellier has demonstrated his thorough knowledge of Nerval scholarship in what may justifiably be called an "état présent des études
nervaliennes." The author brings to our attention such important topics as
Nerval's theatre, the Romanticism of Nerval, the influence of *Wilhelm Meister*
and *Robert le Diable*, "l'Univers de Nerval," etc., few of which have been adequately studied. He contends that "l'oeuvre de Nerval doit être étudiée dans
un ordre strictement chronologique, et selon la méthode de M. Audiat (7),
systématiquement appliquées, ne doit être négligé aucun état du mythe." Pages
28–32 offer a valuable listing and résumé of works by major "Nervaliens
d'aujourd'hui."

66. ———. "Le Romantisme et le mythe d'Orphée." *Cahiers de l'Association Internationale des Etudes Françaises*, no. 10 (mai 1958), 138–57.

On Nerval's adaptation of the Orpheus myth in "El Desdichado," *Les Filles du Feu, Voyage en Orient*, and *Aurélia*. Cellier points out in Court de Gebelin the expression "descente aux enfers" and discusses the relationship between Orpheus' descent and Nerval's spiritual initiation. He further links the theme with Fabre d'Olivet, as well as with *La Flute enchantée*, where Tamino, like Orpheus, is initiated into the rites of Isis.

67. ———. "Sur un vers des *Chimères*." *Cahiers du Sud*, 311 (1952), 146–53.

This extremely influential study offers first a general analysis of the line "Suis-je Amour ou Phébus? . . . Lusignan ou Biron?" from "El Desdichado." Admitting possible multiple meanings behind the names, Cellier establishes certain analogies between the appellations by setting up a chart of other names, such as Alexandre-César . . . Dante-Shakespeare; Cain-Abel . . . Don Juan-Don Quichotte, etc. He reinforces his theory of name-parallels by further studying the duality of Nerval's personality. He opposes, for example, the names Lusignan and Phébus, the former signifying for the poet "dark (night)," the latter "light (day)." The same duality exists in the case of Biron-Lusignan, which leads him to the second part of the article and his interpretation of "Biron" in terms of the figure by the same name in Shakespeare's *Love's Labor's Lost*. In general Cellier sees the poem as a revelation of two types of love: *l'amour fatal, nocturne*, and *l'amour pur, ensoleillé*, both of which correspond in an opposing fashion.

68. Cernuda, Luis. *Poesia y literatura II*. Barcelona: Seix Barral, 1965. 277p.

Contains an excellent essay on Nerval, one of the best in the book, according to the *TLS*: "Like his admired exemplar Nerval, he [Cernuda] romanticized what he found. . . ."

   a. *Times Literary Supplement* (July 8, 1965), 580.

69. Chabrier, René. "Notes sur la structure d'*Aurélia*." *Dialogues*, no. 2 (janv. 1951), 126–33.

The *récit* is studied in terms of its spiritual "mouvement," which, contrary to the belief of most commentators (see in particular 22), suggests little progression. Nerval terminates the work for the sake of its unity, but "il n'y a pas à proprement parler une progression, il y a déroulement, extension, évolution." Discussing the structure first in the light of its artistic merit and second in terms of the poetic portrayal of Man, the author concludes: "*Aurélia* échappe partiellement à la critique logique parce que . . . son message fait appel à la toute-puissance d'un principe insaisissable par les méthodes scientifiques, au principe que Platon osait appeler l'AME."

70. Chambers, Ross. "*Promenades et souvenirs* de Nerval." *Essays in French Literature*, 2 (1965), 43–65.

A general study of the work's major themes and its composition. Depicting "les amours perdues," "la rivalité," and "le double" as the three dominating themes, the author discusses such subtopics as the nostalgia for home life, the image of the rising sun, and Nerval's retrospective voyage into childhood in search of spiritual salvation. As for the work's composition, Chambers speaks of "une simple courbe, spirale virtuelle qui jamais ne se réalise," symbolizing the poet's failure to complete his spiritual voyage.

71. ———. "Une Source nervalienne: la *Sylvie* de Mairet." *Studi Francesi*, XXII (1963), 488–95.

Suggests numerous parallels between Nerval's *Sylvie* and *Promenades et souvenirs* and Mairet's *Sylvie*. Although the author's argument that Gérard found the name for his heroine in this Baroque play is not altogether convincing, his comments on both writers' treatments of the fidelity theme, the "homo duplex," the proper names Myrtil, Philène, and Sylvie, and the theme of time are thought-provoking and persuasive.

72. ———. "Speed and Delay in Nerval." *Australian Journal of French Studies*, I (1964), 40–57.

Drawing primarily from *Voyage en Orient*, *Octavie*, and *Aurélia*, the author discusses the importance of Nerval's travels in his attempt to stabilize a dream world in a life of reality. Reducing "le voyage" to a series of isolated moments, Nerval condenses both time and space in his work. Flight (speed) becomes for the poet exploration, a means by which he can penetrate through reality into the dream. However, because of the prison of time and delay, the poet's search is futile; his escape is illusory.

73. ———. "Water in *Sylvie*." *Modern Language Review*, LVIII, no. 4 (1963), 500–506.

Water in *Sylvie* is interpreted as a "synthetizing principle, combining with air, fire and earth and binding all four together" to unite the work of art. The "water-poetry" of the *nouvelle* helps to reconcile the opposing forces of past and present, reality and the ideal, life and death. Whereas running water suggests life for the poet, stagnant water suggests death, the victory of time, and permanency. Finally, "underlying the theme of love as well as the theme of time, water serves not only to convey the fundamental unity of these two themes but also to suggest by its own ambivalence that the dualism they imply is an illusory one. . . ." The result in *Sylvie* is a "perfect balance where past and present, time and timelessness, reality and the ideal meet and are reconciled."

74. Chase, George, and Pierre Soccane. "Jenny Colon, the Somber Star." *Musical Quarterly*, XXVI (1940), 76–86.

A short biographical sketch that traces the theatrical career of Gérard's heroine.

75. Chouan, Geneviève. "Gérard de Nerval." *Courrier des Marches*, 54 (1959), 15–19; 55–56 (1959), 30–34.

A biographical résumé based on numerous references in Nerval's major works.

76. Christophe, Louis-A. "L'Egypte, Nerval et le daguerréotype." *Revue du Caire*, XXXIX, no. 205 (1957), 211–26.

This excellent study is devoted more to the development of the daguerreotype in Egypt, and Nerval's role in this development than to the poet's literary work.

Posing the question, "[Nerval] était-il . . . le premier voyageur à introduire un daguerréotype en Egypte?" the author traces throughout Gérard's correspondence and the *Voyage en Orient* the various mentions of this photographic technique, pointing out the poet's fascination with the invention and his failure to work out correctly the scientific process. Christophe notes that "Maxime du Camp est le premier voyageur qui ait rapporté d'Egypte une collection de clichés parfaitement réussis" and that not until 1850 was this process of the daguerreotype known as photography.

77. ———. "Gérard de Nerval au Caire." *Revue du Caire*, XXXVI, no. 189 (1956), 171–97.

Concentrates on Nerval's journey to Egypt and clarifies a number of points overlooked by Gilbert Rouger (in his critical edition of the *Voyage en Orient*) and Kléber Haedens (both of whom Christophe attacks in a rather presumptuous and unjustifiable manner). Insisting on the influence on Gérard of Lane's *The Manners and Customs of the Modern Egyptians* (and overlooking the probable fact that the poet did not read English at all well), he devotes considerable attention to Nerval's distorted account of the "cérémonie des oignons," the Pharaoh, and his descriptions of Cham-en-nessim. Nerval apparently never attended an exorcism, though he probably did witness the ceremony of the Evil Eye and the ritual burning of alum. The latter part of the study treats the magical-religious role of the divine onion in Egyptian lore and the manner by which Nerval transformed its meaning in the chapter of *Voyage en Orient* entitled "Les Afrites." The general comments on the poet's "exorcisme" are of interest and lead the author to the following conclusion: "Pour étoffer la trame romanesque de son récit, il ne craint pas de modifier la nature et le déroulement des scènes qu'il décrit ou l'origine et la vie antérieure de ses personnages."

78. ———. "Gérard de Nerval et l'expédition de Richard Lepsius." *Revue du Caire*, XLIV (1960), 44–60.

Nerval's reference in *Les Femmes du Caire* to a certain German companion of Richard Lepsius (the Prussian leader of an expedition into Egypt in 1842) is simply another example of the poet's fabrication of facts and invention of characters. While the actual expedition entered Egypt to explore the pyramids of Gizeh and Saqqara some months before Gérard's arrival, "Nerval souhaitait certainement s'enfoncer à l'intérieur de la grande Pyramide en compagnie de l'un de ces Allemands pour lesquels il n'y a pas de frontière entre le rêve et la réalité." The German companion did not exist. In reality, Nerval is referring to his own friend, Abekem, who was with neither Lepsius nor the other members of the Prussian mission and who himself was probably not able to read to Gérard the hieroglyphic information left by Lepsius. Gérard's account of the expedition was distorted by his imagination.

79. ———. "Les Reliques égyptiennes de Gérard de Nerval." *Revue du Caire*, XXXVI, no. 190 (1956), 51–62. [A continuation of 77.]

A rather superficial analysis of the image of the rose and the symbolic value of its various colors in Nerval's work. Roses in general are related to love ("Chanson gothique" and *Fragments d'un manuscrit d'Aurélia*); "Roses et vigne" concerns the beloved who is married (*Sylvie* and "El Desdichado"); "roses violettes" suggest protective or maternal love (*Octavie* and "Artémis"); "roses pâles" symbolize death (*Octavie*); "rose tremière" has the power to raise the beloved from the abyss ("Artémis" and *Aurélia*); and "roses blanches" symbolize Christian purity ("Artémis"). Concluding the first section, the author adds: ". . . il faut penser, en se fondant sur la description de la comtesse de Gasparin, que le poète cueillit en Egypte une rose de tous les mois." In a second part, he benefits from Durry's *Gérard de Nerval et le mythe* (121) in suggesting further nebulous ideas on the rose imagery.

80. Clancier, Georges-Emmanuel. *De Chénier à Baudelaire: panorama critique.* Paris: Seghers, 1963. 442p. [Coll. "Melior."]

Chapter IV includes general remarks on Nerval and, in particular, the observations published in 81.

a. *Bulletin Critique de Livre Français*, XIX, no. 1 (1964), 5–6.

81. ———. "Notes romantiques; 'Gérard de Nerval ou l'alchimie de l'enfance.'" *Mercure de France*, CCCXLV (1962), 628–33.

An intimate evaluation of the major themes in Nerval's work and the means by which the poet transformed childhood memories into the mature work of art. The author offers also a short commentary on the difference between Nervalian and Proustian techniques.

82. Clouard, Henri. *La Destinée tragique de Gérard de Nerval.* Paris: Bernard Grasset, 1929. 254p.

This mediocre biography, like many others before 1940, views Nerval primarily as the "hero" poet. A phrase from the introductory "Lettre à M. A. Marie" suggests the author's main concern: "Mais ce que je m'étonne qu'aucun nervalien n'ait vu, c'est que le poète hardi et misérable n'a presque pas cessé de frissonner sous la ménace" (p. xi).

83. Coèle, René-Thomas. "La Famille de Jenny Colon." *Revue d'Histoire du Théâtre*, VIII (1956), 50–51.

Discusses in general the theatrical activity of the Colon family and, in particular, Jenny's work at the Théâtre du Havre under the director Dharmeville.

84. Coeuroy, André. *Appels d'Orphée.* Paris: La Nouvelle Revue Critique, 1925. 219p.

Pages 25–91 contain opinions on "Gérard de Nerval musicien." Of especial interest is the author's commentary (pp. 70–76) on Nerval's talent as a music critic.

85. Cogny, Pierre. "Gérard de Nerval aux portes du mystère d'après sa correspondance." *Tour Saint-Jacques*, 13–14 (1958), 47–54.

Stating that a study of a poet's personal correspondence takes on greater significance "quand il s'agit d'un malade, qui a connu son mal, en a souffert, l'a confessé et n'en a jamais été véritablement guéri," the author investigates Nerval's participation in Freemasonry and his interpretation of the dream world, as seen in his letters.

86. Cohn, Norman. "Gérard de Nerval." *Horizon*, IX–XIV (1944–46), 119–38.

A study of the relationship between Nerval's psychopathic experience and his ability to create a work of art. An attentive analysis of *Aurélia* leads to the conclusion that "[the poet's] whole life [and work] was an effort to achieve a compromise between his sexuality and the power within him that condemned it. The structure of his schizophrenia, his sexual mysticism itself, was dictated by this need."

87. Coléno, Alice. *Les Portes d'ivoire: métaphysique et poésie*. Paris, Plon, 1948. 249p.

Gérard de Nerval is joined with Baudelaire, Rimbaud, and Mallarmé in this long study devoted to the poetic experience of the four authors. In her attempt to analyze the works of the poets and demonstrate the very close, personal link between all four, Coléno remarks: "Si Nerval et Rimbaud furent avant tout visionnaires, Baudelaire et Mallarmé artistes, ils ont tous quatre, avec des armes différentes, pénétré dans les mêmes régions mystérieuses . . ." (p. 13).

88. Constans, François. "Une Apocalypse: le sonnet 'A Madame Aguado.' " *Revue des Sciences Humaines*, Fasc. 94 (1959), 275–305.

See 97.

89. ———. "Artémis ou les fleurs du désespoir." *Revue de Littérature Comparée*, XIV (1934), 337–71.

In this exhaustive study of the sonnet "Artémis," the author demonstrates how most of the poem's imagery and symbolism can be traced in Hoffmann's novel *Elixiere des Teufels* (*Elixirs du Diable*). While the article is concerned primarily with a detailed analysis of "Artémis," Constans makes interesting observations on "Antéros" and *Aurélia*, the latter of which he feels was inspired more by Hoffmann's *Elixiere* than by his *Vampire*.

90. ———. "Ascendance mystique: existences mythiques." *Mercure de France*, CCCXVI (1952), 449–61.

An analysis of Nerval's mythomania, based on the poet's "Note généalogique" and the many personages, real or mythical, with whom he identified himself. An important relationship is established between the figures of Joseph Bonaparte, the "Prince de Condé," Sophie de Feuchères, and the concept of the "napoléonide." In reference to "Suis-je Amour ou Phébus? . . . Lusignan ou Biron?" of "El Desdichado" and the theme of "le Double" (or "l'autre"), the author points out that Nerval "*vit* sous toutes ses formes le mythe séculaire de l'Amour et de la Mort." Works primarily considered are "La Tête armée," "El Desdichado," *Pandora*, and *Octavie*.

91. ———. "*Aurélia* ou l'itinéraire de la délivrance," in *Aurélia ou le rêve et la vie* (édition critique de Jean Richer). Paris: Minard, 1965, pp. 251–87.

A rich, comprehensive essay that strives to define and describe once and for all the over-all artistic unity of *Aurélia*. The article is, in reality, an exhaustive *explication de texte* and takes into consideration every possible level on which the *récit* might be interpreted and by which it might be more thoroughly appreciated. Expressing the opinion that *"Aurélia . . .* n'est pas un retour objectif vers le passé; c'est, à l'occasion de ce retour, un jaillissement renouvelé d'émois," Constans investigates empathically the great poetic dream world of Nerval, the illusions and fantasies, the realities, hopes, and miseries; and he shows how the poet, projecting his own real image into a world of myth, sought out and perhaps realized in the work of art the purification of his soul through love.

92. ———. "Daphné et le retour des Dieux." *Revue des Sciences Humaines*, Fasc. 91 (1958), 381–96.

See 97.

93. ———. "Deux enfants du Feu: La Reine de Saba et Nerval." *Mercure de France*, CCCII, no. 1016 (1948), 623–32; CCCII, no. 1017 (1948), 43–54.

Traces the theme of revolt in the *Voyage en Orient, Les Chimères*, and *Octavie*, treating such ideas as "le volcan," "le feu souterrain," "la maîtresse du Feu," and "les fils et les filles du Feu." Included is an admirable interpretation of the sonnet "Myrtho," in which, according to Constans, Nerval demonstrates his overwhelming desire to dominate the element of fire.

94. ———. "Horus et l' 'enfant du miracle.' " *Revue des Sciences Humaines*, Fasc. 94 (1959), 275–305.

See 97.

95. ———. "Nerval et l'amour platonique." *Mercure de France*, CCCXXIV, no. 1101 (1955), 97–119.

A very complex but carefully worked out analysis of *La Pandora*, which Constans sees as "la confession déguisée d'un platonisme exalté de lourdes angoisses." An attentive examination of the major Nervalian themes, dreams, and myths in the short story leads the author to the conclusion that the Platonic elements of the work help not only to define its mystic and moral aspects but also to unify Gérard's amorous and spiritual aspirations.

96. ———. "Le 'Panorama' de Gérard de Nerval," in *Aurélia ou le rêve et la vie* (édition critique de Jean Richer). Paris: Minard, 1965, pp. 289–98.

Attempts to decipher and explain the strange allusions in Nerval's "Voyage d'Italie. Panorama" by studying parallel aspects in the poet's other works. The author depicts three major themes that would appear to define the whole picture portrayed in the "Panorama": (1) "l'enfant mystérieux et [les] naissances singulières"; (2) "[les] hypogées"; (3) "[les]vieillards et [les] Frères, 'amoureux tous deux de la Reine [de Saba].' "

97. ———. "Sibylles nervaliennes"; I. "Daphné et le retour des Dieux," *Revue des Sciences Humaines*, Fasc. 91 (1958), 381–96; II, III. "Horus et l' 'enfant du miracle' " and "Une Apocalypse: le sonnet 'A Madame Aguado,' " *Revue des Sciences Humaines*, Fasc. 94 (1959), 275–305.

The first part of this long and extremely concentrated study is devoted to the sonnet "Delfica" (originally published in 1845 as "Vers dorés") and to its mythological and classical sources. Pointing out Virgil's *Bucolics* and Cicero's

Dream of Scipio, the author discusses at some length the Pythagorean symbolism of the sonnet, linking certain symbols with the imagery of "Myrtho," "Antéros," and *Octavie*. He suggests the possible influence on Nerval of Jean-Pierre Rossignol's *Virgile et Constantin le Grand* and states that "les dieux antiques ne cessent de surgir de la lumière méditerranéenne, et les rêves d'harmonieuse et pure beauté attachés à leurs noms et à leurs légendes, l'attrait exercé par les mythes et les mystères helléniques sur une imagination nourrie de souvenirs classiques et de lectures érudites, tout concourait à le jeter dans une véritable 'ivresse.' " The same exhaustive method of explication is applied in Part II to the sonnet "Horus" and in Part III to "A Madame Aguado." In discussion of the former, Constans notes that "la figure d'Isis était le centre où devaient fatalement converger et se concilier ces divers courants d'idées, de sentiments et de songeries," and he insists that the sonnet be approached in terms of the relationship between collective myth and personal mythology. "A Madame Aguado" (which must be studied in the light of its sister sonnet, "Erythréa") is considered to be primarily an alchemical sonnet that evokes the sibyl of Dies Irae, "celle qui prédit la réduction finale de l'univers temporel en cendres embrasées."

98. ———. "Le Soleil noir et l'Etoile ressuscitée." *Tour Saint-Jacques*, 13–14 (1958), 35–46.

This complex interpretation of the two images takes into account the alchemical and astrological implications suggested by Richer and others. The author contends that "pas plus que le Tombeau, le Soleil noir n'est pour Nerval l'image de la Mort, moins encore celle du Néant"; rather it is "une Réalité négatrice, une Puissance surnaturelle, effrayante de monstrueuse et inhumaine énormité, un Ahriman de l'Occident conçu en figure d'astre." In direct antithesis to this negative image of "El Desdichado," "Le Christ aux Oliviers," *Aurélia*, and *Voyage en Orient* is the accompanying and opposing figure of the *Etoile*, which, symbolizing initially Jenny Colon, then the multiple unity of the Virgin-the Mother-the *Bien-Aimée*, becomes "un gage d'espérance chrétienne" and ultimately, in *Aurélia*, the divine light of universal redemption.

99. ———. "Sophie, Aurélia, Artémis." *Mercure de France*, CCCXII, no. 1054 (1951), 267–81.

An astute analysis of the figure of Sophie, Gérard's "grande amie," the immortal amazon who exercises, in the "Mémorables," "les pouvoirs du Juge céleste . . . et pardonne à Gérard et au monde entier." Pointing out the semidivine significance of the name among the Greeks and the Gnostics, Constans demonstrates the means by which Nerval linked this figure with those of Jenny Colon, Artémis, and Aurélia. He further relates this composite feminine ideal with Sainte Rosalie and Sainte Philomène.

100. ———. "Sur la pelouse de Mortefontaine." *Cahiers du Sud*, XXVIII, no. 292 (1948), 397–412.

In his consideration of "la divine *Sylvie*," Constans centers his attention upon the Valois and its influence not only on *Sylvie* but on all of Gérard's later works. It was at Mortefontaine, Châalis, Ermenonville, etc. that the poet's personal myth began, a myth that was to be reflected both in his works and in the formation of his "image." "Les hameaux, les villages, les sites dont les noms servent de titres à des chapitres successifs: Loisy, Othys, Ermenonville, les brumes de leur ciel, leurs prés, leurs bois, leurs eaux, la poésie de leur passé, les souvenirs qui y surgissent, les rêves qui y naissent, autant de consolateurs." Reflected in this setting is the great image of Woman, a composite figure (Sylvie-Adrienne-Aurélia-Jenny Colon) that gives substance to the poet's artistic creation and spiritual revelation. While *Sylvie* best demonstrates the "Valois du passé," *Promenades et souvenirs* and *Pandora* show a higher level of development in the poet's feminine ideal.

101. ———. *"Sylvie* et ses énigmes." *Revue des Sciences Humaines*, Fasc. 106 (1962), 237–50.

While in his superb article, "Sur la pelouse de Mortefontaine" (100), the author studied the major themes, images, and symbols of *Sylvie*, his intention here is less formal: ". . . rechercher quelle étape du cheminement spirituel de l'auteur constitue cet ouvrage et . . . replacer ce rêve quasi-intemporel dans la chaîne temporelle d'événements intérieurs dont fut faite la vie du rêveur." An attentive investigation of the story and its spiritual and poetic relationships with *La Pandora, Octavie,* and *Aurélia* leads to the following conclusion: "Le cheminement latent auquel ont contribué, à l'occasion d'une grave crise morale, le trouble de la conscience, un platonisme avoué et l'élan religieux de l'âme, c'est le vrai secret de *Sylvie.*"

102. Coppier, André-Charles. "Le Soleil noir de la mélancolie." *Mercure de France*, CCXCIII (1939), 607–10.

Points out that the "Soleil noir" that Gérard noticed in Dürer's *Melancholia I* is no sun at all but the comet that appeared in 1513–1514. Because of its inclination "Dürer a tracé l'image de la comète et de son rayonnement par des traits obscurs, justifiant, jusqu'à un certain point, la magnifique antithèse du 'Soleil noir' d' 'El Desdichado.' "

103. Cottin, Madelaine. "Du nouveau sur la folie de Gérard." *Nouvelles Littéraires* (18 janv. 1962), 1.

A brief commentary on the text of *Aurélia* published in this issue by Jean Porcher (271). The author notes that ". . . ces fragments manuscrits apportent des données nouvelles, témoignage de Nerval lui-même, sur les circonstances qui précédèrent ou vinrent accompagner la première de ses crises de folie assez graves pour nécessiter un internement."

104. Daumal, René. *Chaque fois que l'aube paraît.* Paris: Gallimard, 1953.

Contains a reprint of 105.

105. ———. "Nerval le nyctalope." *Le Grand Jeu* (automne 1930).

The ancient tradition of a "monde intermédiaire" and of "la métamorphose de la conscience" was inherent in Gérard's thought, as was the concept that the entity, the "tout," is constructed from both the visible and invisible worlds, as the *double* was a single being existing on two distinct planes. The author traces an outline of Nerval's *double*, a psychic aspect that was, in a voluntary way, controlled by reason, but that was so essential for the poet's "épreuves initiatrices."

106. Dédéyan, Charles. *Gérard de Nerval et l'Allemagne*. Paris: Société d'édition d'enseignement supérieur, 1957–1959. 3 vols. [I: *La Formation: l'Allemagne dans la vie de Gérard de Nerval*; II: *La Création: l'Allemagne dans l'oeuvre littéraire de Nerval*; *La Vocation: l'Allemagne dans la mystique nervalienne*; III: *Textes inédits et introuvables*.]

The first volume of this monumental work is a biographical study of the poet and of the influence of Germany on his life and personality. Particular emphasis is placed on Gérard's translations of such German poets as Goethe, Hoffmann, Kotzebue, and Heine. In the second volume (by far more valuable than the first), the author proposes to "étudier en fonction des jugements de Gérard de Nerval sur la littérature allemande, les affinités électives qui se précisent dans le choix des auteurs, le choix des oeuvres et le choix des thèmes" (p. 270). He investigates at great length Nerval's poetic imitations of Heine, the presence of Hoffmann in the poet's "contes fantastiques," and, above all, the influence of Goethe and Klinger on Gérard's literary creation. The third part of the study, "La Vocation" — the title of which is not included in the title page of Volume II — treats Nerval's mystic affinities with Novalis, Creuzer, Böttiger, and Boehme. Dédéyan includes in his consideration the images of *la mère*, *la grotte*, *le bain*, and *la fleur*, as well as the Nervalian themes of universal harmony, *correspondances*, syncretism, and *le monde souterrain*. The general conclusion is significant: "L'Allemagne . . . qui l'enchante, ces décors d'opéra et d'opérette du Rhin et de la Bavière ou même de Vienne, devient de plus en plus la Terre de l'Au-delà, le lieu où l'on a le droit de vivre son rêve et de rêver sa vie, où un peu de folie . . . ne gâte rien à l'affaire et passe pour de l'inspiration. C'est à cette Allemagne que dans les affres de l'Agonie avant l'appel suprême de la mort, Gérard va demander consolation et réconfort. L'Allemagne est en un sens . . . sa mystique consolatrice" (pp. 659–60). Volume III — incorrectly classified as the third part of the general study — includes no more than photographic reproductions of four unpublished plays by Nerval (?): *Misanthropie et repentir*, *Nicholas Flamel-Le Rêve et la vie*, *L'Imagier de Harlem*, and *L'Alchimiste*.

    a. J.-P. Attal. *Critique*, XVI (1960), 571–72.

    b. H. Petit. "De Mme. de Staël à Nerval." *Nouvelles Littéraires* (3 sept. 1959), 2–3.

    c. R. Pouilliart. *Lettres Romanes*, XVII, no. 3 (1963), 295–97.

    d. D. Rasmussen. *Erasmus*, XII (1960), 279–83.

107. ———. *Le Thème de Faust dans la littérature européenne*. Paris: Les Lettres Modernes, 1954–57. 3 vols.

Volume III includes a chapter on Nerval's translation of *Faust* and the general influence of Faustian themes in his major work.

108. ———. "Vocation faustienne de Gérard de Nerval." *Revue des Lettres Modernes*, IV, nos. 25–26 (1957), 49–98.

For the reader who is unable to consult either Vol. I of 106 or Vol. III of 107, this article offers an admirable résumé of the Faustian elements in Nerval's work. Although the essay is condensed, the author touches on such important topics as "Le Second *Faust*," "Le Créateur faustien," "Marguerite perdue," "Nerval et la légende de Faust," "*L'Imagier de Harlem*," and "Le Vrai *Faust*."

109. Deharme, Lise. "Lord Pilgrim." *Tour Saint-Jacques*, 13–14 (1958), 32–34.

A note of little importance, concerned mainly with the author's personal impressions of the poet. One interesting observation: "Nerval — nerval — corne d'une licorne qui hante Paris, chaque fois que nous glanons l'étrange dans des promenades solitaires."

110. Delay, Jean. "Autour d'*Aurélia*." *Nouvelles Littéraires* (29 mai 1958), 1, 6.

A psychological interpretation of Gérard's dream world. To study *Aurélia* as a clinical document helps in no way to explain the mystery of the *récit*. The art of the piece rests in Nerval's poetic "rapports entre le rêve et le délire," which enabled him to transcend the oneiric universe of a madman.

111. Derché, Roland. "Explication de texte: Gérard de Nerval." *Information Littéraire* (mars–avril 1957). [Reprinted in *Etudes de textes français*. Paris: Société d'édition d'enseignement supérieur, 1959.]

An explication of *Aurélia*, "Première partie," VI–VIII.

112. Dhaevens, Jacques. "A propos de l'établissement du texte de 'El Desdichado.' " *Studi Francesi*, X (1966), 286–89.

Points out the three existing versions of the sonnet: the original publication in *Le Mousquetaire* (10 déc. 1853), the Eluard manuscript, and the Lombard manuscript, and attempts to establish by means of chronology the date of the original composition.

113. DuBruck, Alfred J. *Gérard de Nerval and the German Heritage*. The Hague: Mouton, 1965. 136p.

An interesting and original study of the artistic and intellectual relationship between Nerval and Hoffmann, Goethe, and Heine. While the second chapter deals with Gérard's work (especially the *Doppelgänger* motif), and the third chapter appraises Nerval's use of the *Faust* theme, Chapter IV concentrates on the extent to which Gérard was influenced by Heine's emotional lyricism. The author concludes that German literature served both to improve the poet's stylistic techniques and to intensify his depth of perception in the artistic description of emotional states. Although the title of the introductory chapter, "*Etat présent* of Nerval Studies," may be misleading (the material covers mainly the studies on Nerval's Germanism), this short discussion on bibliography will be found extremely useful, as will the listing of critical studies in the Bibliography at the end.

114. ———. "More on Nerval's 'Benoni.' " *Romance Notes*, VI, no. 2 (1965), 121.

Points out Jean Richer's note in the second Pléiade edition (1961) of the *Oeuvres*, which suggests as a source for the name "Ben-oni" (Hebrew for "son of my suffering") Genesis 35:18. (cf. 55 and 116)

115. ———. "Nerval's *Léo Burckart*: Message or Confession." *Romanic Review*, LVI, no. 4 (1965), 262–71.

The most thorough discussion of a play which "unequivocally . . . deserves a place in anthologies with *Ruy Blas*, *Fantasio*, and *Chatterton*." Comparing in detail the original version of 1838 (written in collaboration with Dumas) and Nerval's revision of 1839, the author demonstrates how Nerval, through numerous dramatic and character changes, added to the play artistic qualities that a popularizer like Dumas could never have conceived. Showing, further, how Gérard used *Léo Burckart* to express his personal emotions and recollections, DuBruck concludes that the play is personal, not political: "The political issues, even though they form the frame of the plot, are and remain of lesser significance."

116. ———. "A Source for Nerval's 'Benoni.' " *Romance Notes*, IV, no. 2 (1963), 117–18.

The name "Benoni," the protagonist's chief aid in the *Histoire de la Reine du Matin* (*Voyage en Orient*), may have been taken from the name of Pétrus Borel's brother. (cf. 55 and 114)

117. Duckworth, Colin. "Eugène Scribe and Gérard de Nerval: 'Celui qui tient la corde nous étrangle.' " *Modern Language Review*, LX, no. 1 (1965) 32–40.

An interesting article that, if nothing else, significantly draws into closer perspective the theatrical relationship between Nerval, Méry, and Scribe. The author is concerned primarily with Philibert Audebrand's libelous campaign against Scribe in 1859, when the former accused Scribe of "causing" the death of Nerval and produced a letter from Nerval to Méry that he felt would prove his case. That Scribe was found innocent supports the impression that, though Gérard had reason to envy Scribe's overrated success in the theatre, he nevertheless respected the playwright's talents as a librettist for opera and comic opera. If anyone expressed a malicious and revengeful attitude toward Scribe, it was none other than Audebrand and the pompous Méry. Duckworth suggests, further, that "if Gérard had only lowered himself to writing a play in collaboration with Scribe . . . , the amalgamation of poetry, wit, and good dramatic technique might have produced the great *drame complet* that the Romantics never managed to create."

118. Ducray, Camille. *Gérard de Nerval*. Paris: Jules Tallandier, 1946. 301p.

This biography, divided into three parts ("L'Eveil," "Le Rêve," and "La Mort"), represents a sincere attempt to place Nerval in his proper poetic inheritance and to "dégager l'influence de son caractère sur son oeuvre et de son oeuvre sur sa vie" (p. 8). The work is well documented with the poet's works, along with numerous texts by Gérard's contemporaries. Notes and a glossary are included at the end.

119. Dumont, Francis. "Gérard avant Nerval." *Nouvelles Littéraires* (29 mai 1958), 7.

One of the few items to treat Nerval's youthful political activity. Noting that Gérard was imprisoned twice after the Revolution of 1830, the author supposes that "[il] tourna le dos à l'opposition dès que la Monarchie de Julliet se montra sévère aux bousingots et autres républicains. . . ." However, Gérard was always conscious of social justice and alludes to it throughout his work.

120. Durry, Marie-Jeanne. "De quelques images." *Tour Saint-Jacques*, 13–14 (1958), 88–90.

Comments on Nerval's Pythagorean attachment to "la pierre" and its symbolic relation to the sun: "Ce soleil qu'il aime, d'une autre manière encore il l'a capté dans la pierre."

121. ———. *Gérard de Nerval et le mythe*. Paris: Flammarion, 1956. 204p.

Contending that the most valuable reading of Nerval is a simple one, the author concentrates her attention on the poetic development of myth and finds in such early pieces as "La Grand'mère" the initial "creusement." The myth is created by substituting a collective mental awareness of things for an individual awareness, whereby an "universalisation du souvenir" is achieved. In this development, aspects such as esotericism are simply undefined means in the art of creation and are significant only to the extent that they contribute to the creative process. Durry demonstrates the creation of personal myth in the *Histoire du Calife Hakem*, the *Songe de Poliphile*, *Aurélia*, *Sylvie*, and *Les Chimères*. In all these works reigns "le souvenir," viewed as an aspect of permanence that actually exists no longer but whose substance gives ground to the poetic myth. "En vérité, rien ne compte pour Nerval que ceci: parvenir à la certitude de l'immortalité et de la coexistence de toutes les personnes aimées" (p. 145). [See Jeanine Moulin's excellent review article: "Gérard de Nerval et le mythe," *Bulletin de l'Académie Royale de Langue et de Littérature Française*, no. 3 (1957), 189–93. (246)]

    a. R.-M. Albérès. *Revue des Sciences Humaines* (1956), 359–61.
    b. H. Amer. *Cahiers du Sud*, XLIII, no. 336 (1956), 317–18.
    c. C. Borgal. *Monde Nouveau-Paru*, XI, no. 104 (1956), 64–70.
    d. H. Clouard. *La Table Ronde*, no. 102 (1956), 176–78.
    e. R. Jean. *Cahiers du Sud*, XLIII, no. 339 (1957), 312–14.
    f. R. Lacoste. *Lettres Françaises*, no. 658 (1957), 3.
    g. J. Madaule. *Le Monde*, IX, no. 400 (1956), 4.
    h. P. Moreau. *Revue de Littérature Comparée* (1956), 576–78.
    i. E. Noulet. *Lettres Nouvelles*, IV, no. 2 (1956), 479–81.
    j. P. Pia. *Carrefour*, XIII, no. 639 (1956), 9.
    k. L. Thompson. *Kentucky Foreign Language Quarterly*, IV (1957), 164–69.
    l. P. Jourda. *Revue des Langues Modernes*, LXXII (1956), 227.

122. Eco, Umberto. "Il Tempo di *Sylvie*." *Poesia e Critica*, I (1961), 51–66.

Defining the novella as "una manomissione del tempo," the author shows how, otherwise than in the work of Proust — who actually identified, described, and attempted to develop the time element — in *Sylvie* "il gioco della memoria non viene 'descritto' o 'affermato,' ma si instaura nella stessa struttura del racconto identificandosi con essa." With no set plan, Nerval distributes his personages within an undefined period of time, to such a degree that the reader begins to recognize not chaos but a type of stability in time and "un certo modo di videre e di patire il mondo." A table is established whereby the temporal quality of the work may be viewed on eight different levels. The author concludes that time in *Sylvie* gradually begins to define an ultimate tragedy and thus becomes itself a prelude to death.

123. Engler, Winfried. *Der französische Roman von 1800 bis zur Gegenwart.* Sammlung Dalp, 1965. 299p.

Chapter III, "Phantastische Erzählung und phantastischer Roman," includes a résumé of and commentary on Gérard's fantastic short stories.

124. Engstrom, Alfred G. "Gérard de Nerval's Lobster and the Tarot Cards." *Romance Notes*, VI, no. 1 (1964), 33–36.

Points out Card XVIII, "La Lune," in the Greater Arcana of the Tarot as containing the explanation of Gérard's famous reference to the lobster that does not swallow the human monad like a dog. Seeing the reproduction of the card in Court de Gebelin's *Monde primitif* (1781), which shows a crab-like creature rising from the waters and two dogs barking at the moon or snapping at its emanations, Nerval identified the strange scene with an androgynous reference to Isis in Plutarch's "Isis and Osiris" in the *Moralia.*

125. ———. "The 'Horus' of Gérard de Nerval." *Philological Quarterly*, XXXIII, no. 1 (1954), 78–80.

Sees the sonnet as a statement of personal mysticism and religious syncretism based on an essential life-force (represented by "Isis, la mère") from which new life comes. The eagle is possibly a symbol of religious syncretism (or mythical incarnation), as well as of keen-eyed vision, which actuates the great Life-Principle in the universe. The author makes the observation that the first and last letters of each line in the first quatrain spell out the key to the poem: LIFE SEES.

126. Ernest-Charles, J. "Gérard de Nerval et l'Allemagne." *Revue Politique et Littéraire*, LXII (1905), 247–50.

In this portrait of Nerval as a pure classicist living in the Romantic period, the author attributes little importance to German influence on the poet's artistic creation.

127. Fabre, Jean. *Les Flandres dans les mouvements romantiques et symbolistes.* Paris: Actes du Second Congrès Nationale de la Société Française de Littérature Comparée, 1958.

The only study devoted to the general influence of the Netherlands on Nerval and to the poet's search in this geographical area for "un paysage intérieur." See pp. 61–73, "Nerval et les Flandres."

128. Fairlie, Alison. "An Approach to Nerval," in *Studies in Modern French Literature* (presented to P. Mansell Jones). Manchester: The University Press, 1961, pp. 87–103.

This admirable commentary provides a most valuable introduction to Nerval for nonspecialists dismayed by what the author terms the "débauche d'herméneutique." In no way neglecting current research, Fairlie takes what she considers Gérard's two major works, *Les Chimères* and *Sylvie*, and demonstrates how there emerge from these masterpieces "a worthwhile meaning and an art which make Nerval neither just the poet of the music-makers nor the delight of the juggler with cryptograms and crossword-puzzles" (p. 89). An excellent discussion (*explication de texte*) of the sonnets in "Le Christ aux Oliviers" and of "El Desdichado" is followed by a simple but valid analysis of *Sylvie*, of which Fairlie states generally: "From both the limpingly natural and the elaborately formalized Nerval weaves his sense of tenderness, irony and final persistence" (p. 102).

    a. W. H. Barber. *Modern Language Review*, LVII, no. 3 (1962), 453–54.

    b. R. Fargher. *French Studies*, XVII, no. 1 (1963), 50–51.

129. ———. "Nerval et Richelet." *Revue des Sciences Humaines*, Fasc. 91 (1958), 397–400.

After commenting on the rich musical quality of Nerval's rhyme in the *Chimères*, the author brings to light Richelet's *Dictionnaire de Rimes* (1751), of which Nerval made frequent use. She notes in the dictionary the appearance of such rhymed words as Biron-Achéron, Fée-Orphée, Cocyte-Amalécite, etc., many of which Nerval adapted in creating the *Chimères*.

130. Fouchet, Max-Pol. "Nerval et le dessein du XIXe siècle." *Tour Saint-Jacques*, 13–14 (1958), 8–11.

Though probably not familiar with William Blake, Nerval was "un témoin de l'effondrement de l'ordre traditionnaliste" during the first half of the nineteenth century. The critic comments on the unique quality of Gérard's romanticism, his interest in the eighteenth-century illuminists, and the means by which he was able to create and control "un univers d'archétypes perdus."

131. Fowlie, Wallace. *Love in Literature*. Bloomington: Indiana University Press, 1965. 156p. [Originally published as *The Clown's Grail: A Study of Love in its Literary Expression*. Denver: Alan Swallow, 1948.]

Chapter 3, entitled "Nerval: the Poet's Uncrowning," is basically a study of Nervalian metempsychosis, which, according to the distinguished author, "abolishes, by surpassing it, the tragic notion of love" (p. 61). For Nerval, love *is* metempsychosis, for "it inevitably triumphs over physical experience in binding us to time which has gone by, to a past which becomes present and future" (p. 60). Fowlie's sensitive analyses of the poet's dream world, his position in a motionless time, and his desperate search for pure love demonstrate a remarkable and rare understanding of Gérard.

132. Françon, Marcel. "A Propos du concours d'éloquence (1828), organisé par l'Académie Française." *Studi Francesi*, VI, no. 18 (1962), 487–88.

Insists that Gérard's comic satire, *L'Académie ou les membres introuvables*, was not written against the Academy's decision to award the prize of 1828 to Philarète Charles and Saint-Marc Girardin. The author remarks that there exists no autograph manuscript by Nerval in the Academy archives.

133. ———. "The Attitude of Gérard de Nerval toward Ronsard." *Modern Language Quarterly*, XXII, no. 2 (1961), 153–57.

Between the dates 1830, when Nerval published his *Choix des poésies de Ronsard, DuBellay, Baïf, etc.*, and 1852, when he published his article in *L'Artiste* on "Les Poètes du seizième siècle," his appreciation of and attitude toward Ronsard changed. Françon attributes this in part to the contemporary influence of Friedrich Schlegel, Nodier, and Paul-Louis Courier.

    a. G. Franceschetti. *Studi Francesi*, XVI (1962), 172.

134. ———. "L'Etude de Gérard de Nerval sur les poètes du XVIe siècle." *Studi Francesi*, V, no. 1 (1961), 463–73.

Reproduces another version of Nerval's study on the Renaissance poets: the text that appeared in 1852 in *L'Artiste*, the only one "dans lequel on puisse avoir confiance." Françon notes that William Duckett's French translation of Friedrich Schlegel's [German] *History of Ancient and Modern Literature* probably influenced Nerval.

135. ———. [Gérard de Nerval. *L'Académie ou les membres introuvables*. Réproduction photographique de l'édition originale (1826). Cambridge: Schoenhof's, 1961, ii–44 + 45–ivp.]

This edition contains a significant analysis of the text. The author also reaffirms his belief that Nerval was not writing against the Academy in this one-act, three-scene satire (see 132) and that there was no "rancune personnelle de l'auteur à l'égard de l'Académie . . . ou désir de vengeance qu'il aurait eu pour n'avoir pas reçu la récompense à l'occasion du concours organisé pour 1828" (pp. 37–38).

136. ———. "Gérard de Nerval et la poésie populaire." *Bulletin Folklorique d'Ile-de-France*, XXIII (avril–juin 1960), 171, 178.

A very vague commentary on Friedrich Schlegel and the limited influence of his poetic theory on Nerval's conception of "la poésie populaire." Schlegel advocated a return to religious inspiration rather than to popular poetry.

137. ———. "Gérard de Nerval et Paul-Louis Courier." *French Review*, XXXII (1959), 461–62.

Points out the similarity of Courier's and Nerval's ideas on the language in the sixteenth century, as expressed in Nerval's introduction to his *Choix des poésies de Ronsard* . . . and Courier's *Prospectus* to his translation of Herodotus.

138. ———. "Note sur l'étude de Nerval: 'Les Poètes du XVIe siècle.'" *Studi Francesi*, IV (1960), 276–78.

By studying the variants of the early edition of DuBellay's *Défense et illustration*, Françon contends that Nerval, in his study of the Renaissance poet, did not use the original edition of 1549 but that of 1561, edited by Fédéric Morel. After correcting certain errors in Richer's presentation in the *Oeuvres complémentaires* and discussing the conditions under which Nerval composed his study on the Pléiade poets, the author concludes that, if Gérard did take part in the competition of 1828, his "Mémoire" probably had little connection with the introduction he wrote to the *Choix*. Furthermore, unlike Richer, he endorses the "Mémoire" of 1830 as the standard text and not that which appeared in *L'Artiste* in 1852.

139. ———. "A Source of Gérard de Nerval." *Modern Language Review*, LIV (1959), 231–33.

Insists on the influence on Nerval of Friedrich Schlegel and his poetic ideas by pointing out the latter's *Histoire de la littérature ancienne et moderne* as the source of a quotation Nerval included in his introduction to the *Choix des poésies de Ronsard* (1830).

140. ———. "Le Texte de l'étude de Gérard de Nerval sur les poètes du XVIe siècle." *Studi Francesi*, II (1958), 432–34.

Brings together the various theories concerning Nerval's original text (Archetype X) on the Pléiade poets and attempts to establish a schema by which the existing three versions might be collated.

141. Freer, Alan J. "Diderot, *Angélique* et les *Confidences de Nicolas*." *Studi Francesi*, IX (1965), 283–90.

An extremely valuable continuation of Raymond Jean's 1955 study of Diderot's and Sterne's literary influence on Nerval (181). The author notes that, although Gérard did not adhere directly to the narrative tradition established by the authors of *Jacques le fataliste* and *Tristram Shandy*, "il n'en reste pas moins vrai qu'*Angélique* est plein de souvenirs plus ou moins conscients de Diderot, qui évoquent parfois l'écho plus lointain de Sterne." Nerval suggests further his debt to Diderot in his *Confidences de Nicolas*, where he refers the reader to the dialogue and the narrative descriptions in *Le Neveu de Rameau*. Influenced perhaps by Nodier and Jules Janin's critical commentaries on the *Philosophe-romancier*, Nerval — along with Hugo and Musset — is one of the few Romantic prose writers to adopt Diderot as a model, to "passer de l'admiration des romans de Diderot à l'inspiration directe."

142. Fréville, Jacques. "Gérard de Nerval." *Arcadie*, 117 (1963), 416–20; 120 (1963), 583–86.

Claims to reveal from an episode in *Voyage en Orient* Nerval's homosexual tendencies, defined as "les goûts les plus secrets (ou peut-être les mieux cachés) de l'auteur d'*Aurélia* et des lettres à Jenny Colon."

143. Galotti, Jean. "Gérard de Nerval: Der Dichter." *Antares*, III, no. 2 (1955), 50–52.

Discussing the Symbolist nature of Nerval's verse, which anticipated the poetry of Verlaine, Rimbaud, Mallarmé, and Valéry, and noting that "auch die Surrealisten hatten Nerval bereits zu ihrem Vorläufer erklärt," the author speaks of what he calls the "Dunkelheit" of the *Chimères*, which "erscheint uns so schön, das wir gerade darin einen Genuss finden, sie ohne Erklärungen aufzunehmen" and which gave this verse its original and intriguing quality.

144. Gaulmier, Jean. "Le Dernier Espoir de Nerval." *Nouvelles Littéraires* (29 mai 1958), 8.

A study of the mother-image, "qui tourne Gérard vers l'illuminisme." The poet's love of esoteric doctrine was not the result of any philosophic curiosity, but represented for him a means by which he, like Faust, could better penetrate time: ". . . un besoin sentimental, le désir de remonter le temps, de retrouver la jeune mère morte qu'il n'a pas connue. . . ."

145. ———. *Gérard de Nerval et les Filles du Feu*. Paris. Nizet, 1956. 174p.

In this admirable study of *Les Filles du Feu*, the author attempts, while analyzing each of the seven texts, to show the over-all coherence of the col-

lection and the means by which Nerval links his subjects to attain an ultimate unity. He furthermore demonstrates how the stories are related to the
subject matter of the preface to Dumas of the *Chimères*. He concludes that
Gérard was intent on establishing a definite architecture in the collection
and that the mystic value of the number seven was particularly meaningful
to the poet. The final pages are devoted to Gérard's syncretic nature.

    a. J. Kneller. *Romanic Review*, XLIX (1958), 72–73.

    b. C. Pichois. *Revue d'Histoire Littéraire de la France*, LVIII (1958),
       404–6.

146. Gauthier-Ferrières. *Gérard de Nerval: la vie et l'oeuvre*. Paris: Alphonse
      Lemerre, 1906. 350p.

The first serious biographical study on Nerval. Although numerous details
on the poet's life are constructed around romantic legend and are incorrect,
the author's effort to clarify Nerval's position in French letters and to point
out the merits of his major work deserves recognition.

147. Genaille, Jeanne. "Balzac, Nerval et Aguado." *Revue d'Histoire Littéraire
      de la France*, LXI, no. 3 (1961), 389–404.

Points out the figure of the Marquise Alexandre Marie Aguado, whose personality and beauty inspired both Balzac's *Un Début dans la vie* and Nerval's
sonnet "A Madame Aguado" — although the artistic results of the two works
are clearly different. Gérard had numerous occasions to visit the Aguado
family in Paris between 1830 and 1840.

    a. R. Masetti. *Studi Francesi*, XVI (1962), 168.

148. ———. "Sur 'El Desdichado.'" *Revue d'Histoire Littéraire de la France*,
      LX, no. 1 (1960), 1–10.

An unconvincing attempt to link the hero of the sonnet with Richard Coeur
de Lion and to interpret the piece generally in terms of legend and history.
The author contends that each verse expresses "le souvenir transposé d'une
aventure historique ou l'âme du guerrier vaincu [Richard] puis du poète
inspiré." Her contention that the thematic origins of "El Desdichado" are to
be found in the earlier sonnet "A Madame Sand" is quite unacceptable.

149. Geninasca, Jacques. *Une Lecture de "El Desdichado."* Paris: Minard, 1965.
      61p. [Archives des Lettres Modernes (160–163); Archives Nervaliennes, 5.]

The most complete single study of the sonnet up to date. Citing first two
important variants ("des baisers de la reine" and "J'ai dormi dans la grotte")
overlooked by Moulin and Richer, and acknowledging the importance of the
preceding analyses by Kneller (197), Constans (90), Cellier (67), and
Gérard (151), the author points out the ninth verse, "Suis-je Amour ou
Phébus? . . . Lusignan ou Biron?" as the central idea around which the
whole poetic concept revolves: "Il implique l'existence d'une opposition qui
se manifeste aussi bien dans la sphère de *'l'antiquité païenne'* qu'à l'époque
du *'moyen âge chrétien'* " (p. 31). The quatrains, studied in terms of their
temporal symbolism, are united with the tercets by the general theme of
duality. Furthermore: "Leur fonction [celle des tercets] consiste à reprendre
les deux systèmes d'oppositions qui paralysaient les quatrains, à dépasser la
première contradiction (temps historique/espace mythique) et à instituer,

entre les termes de la seconde antinomie ("Apollon"/"Dionysos") un rapport dialectique de complémentarité" (p. 46). Geninasca's ideas tend to be superficial, and his method of explication is at times extremely trying.

150. George, Albert J. *Short Fiction in France, 1800-1850.* Syracuse University Press, 1964. iv + 245p.

Pages 208-16 are devoted to Nerval's important role in the development of short fiction in France. Going beyond the formal concepts of Balzac and Borel, and rejecting the rigid form in which Mérimée had encased the short narrative, Nerval "transformed the conventions he had received in legacy into the possibility of a literary new vision" (p. 216); he changed the form from expository to revelatory. Although this is one of the few studies concerned primarily with Nerval's short fiction, the author's view is distorted by his unawareness of certain essential facts. For example, *Emilie* and *Jemmy* are not by Nerval but are merely translations of Charles Sealsfield and Auguste Maquet. However, George's comments on *La Main enchantée, L'Histoire du Calife Hakem, L'Histoire de la Reine du Matin, La Reine des poissons, La Pandora* (which he misspells *Pandore*!), *Sylvie* and *Aurélia* (misquoted as *Aurélia ou le Rêve*) help to draw some definite perspective on a generally neglected topic.

a. P. Ciureanu. *Studi Francesi,* IX (1965), 166-67.

151. Gérard, Albert S. "Images, structure et thèmes dans 'El Desdichado.'" *Modern Language Review,* LVIII, no. 4 (1963), 507-15.

In this brilliantly developed exegesis, the author approaches the sonnet as a work of art, complete within itself and containing "une signification perceptible sans références excessives à autre chose que lui-même." After correcting Kneller's comments (197) concerning the title of the sonnet, he suggests two initial themes, "la souffrance" and "l'art," the reciprocal relationship of which unifies the poem. The antithetical structure is based on the opposing classical-Mediterranean and Nordic-medieval elements of the piece: *Amour, Phoebus — Lusignan, Biron; Orphée, lyre, Achéron, sirène — sainte, fée, reine, Prince d'Aquitaine,* etc., all of which crystallize and are synthesized into a common essence, thus producing a third and final theme: ". . . l'art transcend la souffrance en immortalisant l'expérience humaine en une 'chose de beauté'; sur un plan esthétique, l'art véritable concilie la plasticité classique et l'intériorité médiévale, anéantissant ainsi les contingences de l'espace et du temps." Without question one of the finest studies devoted to the sonnet.

152. Gerhardt, Mia I. "L'Imagerie de *Sylvie.*" *Neophilologus,* XXXIX (1955), 9-15.

Although this short article includes few original observations with regard to pattern imagery in *Sylvie,* it does offer an interesting analysis of the poetic *ambiance* that exists among the characters, and it demonstrates the manner by which Nerval creates this *ambiance* within the basic framework of symbol and imagery.

153. ———. "L'*Octavie* de Nerval." *Neophilologus,* XLII (1958), 24-30.

Attention is centered first on an acceptable comparison of the general episode in *Octavie* and the similar details offered in the 1837 *Lettre* to Jenny Colon. It is concluded that, while the two texts relate the same personal experience, it would appear that the initial episode of 1834 with the young English girl in Italy (portrayed in *Octavie*) gradually took on new meaning for the poet who, in the *Lettre*, describes Jenny Colon. "Il a constaté plus tard, rétrospectivement, la ressemblance de Jenny avec la brodeuse (comme celle de l' 'actrice' avec Adrienne), et en profite pour donner, dans sa lettre . . . à l'aventure napolitaine une signification qu'elle n'eut pas en réalité." Gerhardt next compares *Sylvie* and *Octavie*, and she contends that "les deux nouvelles forment en quelque sorte un diptyque, la seconde reprenant, avec moins de force et de clarté, dans un décor différent, les thèmes principaux de la première."

154. Gilbert, Judson Bennett, M.D. *Disease and Destiny. A Bibliography of References to the Famous.* London: Dawsons of Pall Mall, 1962. 535p.

Cites twelve medical studies on Nerval, the first dating from 1897 and the last from 1958.

155. Girard, Georges. "Les Sources historiques de l'*Angélique* de Gérard de Nerval." *Opinion* (1927), 13–15.

Introduces the late nineteenth-century bibliophile Auguste Longnon, who established the definitive text of *La Véritable Histoire d'Angélique de Longueval* and whose son Henri later depended on Nerval's *Angélique* in the presentation of the Cité des Livres text. With regard to Gérard's rendition of the story, the author notes "[quel] charme le poète peut ajouter aux histoires les plus charmantes."

156. Giraudoux, Jean. "Gérard de Nerval," in *Littérature*. Paris: Grasset, 1941, pp. 77–87.

Rejecting the thesis of P. Audiat (7), Giraudoux sees *Aurélia* as "une leçon suprême de la poésie" and discusses what he considers the poet's purpose in composing the masterpiece: "En amplifiant, en modelant *Aurélia*, Nerval n'a pas désiré autre chose que de bien préciser à la vie qu'il l'avait comprise."

157. Glatigny, Michel. "*La Main enchantée* de Nerval: quelques sources du XVIIe siècle." *Revue des Sciences Humaines*, Fasc. 119 (1965), 329–52.

The only concentrated study of Nerval's *La Main enchantée*, a short story that the critic feels has been unjustifiably neglected and that without a doubt deserves attention. While analyzing as succinctly as possible the subject matter and structure of the piece, Glatigny points out numerous sources in Montaigne ("Que philosopher, c'est apprendre à mourir"), Cyrano de Bergerac, Bruscambille, Merlin Coccaie, and Furetière, and he demonstrates to what extent Nerval made use of these sources.

158. Goffin, Robert. "Clefs pour Gérard de Nerval." *Figaro Littéraire*, XV (3 déc. 1960), 5, 6.

Pretends to find the key to the sonnet "El Desdichado" in Grétry's opera *Richard Coeur de Lion*, which was presented in Brussels in 1840 and in which Jenny Colon interpreted the leading role of Marguerite, Richard's queen. Goffin relates the symbolic elements of the play to such allusions in Gérard's sonnet as the "Prince d'Aquitaine," the "ténébreux," "Biron," etc. Most of his ideas are quite far-fetched and demonstrate in no way an understanding of the sonnet as a work of art. (cf. 159, Chap. XV.)

159. ———. *Fil d'Ariane pour la poésie.* Paris: Nizet, 1964.

Chapters XIII–XVIII are devoted to Nerval and, more specifically, to the sonnets "El Desdichado," "Artémis," and "Erythréa." While Chapter XV includes the same exegetical material as the author's "Clefs pour Gérard de Nerval," the other essays concentrate on the relationship between the sonnets and Nerval's other work. Establishing "la monomanie amoureuse" as a central theme in *Les Chimères* and pointing out that "tout ce que [Nerval] va exposer dans ces sonnets se trouve déjà dans les *Filles du Feu*, et dans son oeuvre" (p. 87), the author traces in the poet's opus the various possible sources of each line in the three sonnets.

160. Goosse, Marie-Thérèse. "'El Desdichado' de Gérard de Nerval." *Lettres Romanes*, XVIII, no. 2 (1964), 111–35; XVIII, no. 3 (1964), 241–62.

In this lengthy, almost exhaustive explication of the sonnet, the author not only offers a number of original ideas, but she benefits from her admirable knowledge of the multiple analyses that have preceded her article. Her interpretation of the sonnet is perhaps unique in that it is based almost entirely on Nerval's writings and not on exterior influences, sources, etc. "Il m'a semblé que la méthode la meilleure . . . était de rechercher dans les écrits de l'auteur ceux qui pourraient éclairer le sens de ces mots, de ces figures, ou qui conduiraient à des sources, à des références précieuses." She contends first that the essence of the sonnet lies in the title, which must be interpreted in terms of two meanings: "El Desdichado" and "Le Déshérité," both of equal value. Attention is drawn to the importance of Scarron's *Le Roman comique* and to Brantôme, as well as to Nerval's *Le Prince des Sots*, in which the author finds the substance of numerous images and symbols in the sonnet. Although she leans heavily — perhaps justifiably so — on the symbolic allusions in *Aurélia*, Goosse demonstrates equally the related importance of *Voyage en Orient*, *La Pandora*, *Octavie*, *Isis*, *Corilla*, and the poet's introduction to *Faust*. She concludes that the reader perceives in "El Desdichado," as in much of Nerval's work, "la figure de l'espoir."

    a. G. Franceschetti. *Studi Francesi*, IX (1965), 174.

161. Graaf, Daniel-A. de. "Gérard de Nerval traducteur de Henri Heine." *Langues Modernes*, XLIX (1955), 125–29.

A short but interesting note on Gérard's 1848 translation entitled *Les Poésies de Henri Heine* and the commentary that accompanied the translation. Nerval is described as both "un excellent psychologue, doué d'un fin esprit d'analyse" and as the Romantic who depicted and analyzed in Heine's work those poetic elements which would later characterize the verse of Baudelaire and the Symbolists. Furthermore, a careful reading of Gérard's portrait of Heine reveals the French poet's own image, later to be developed in the *Chimères* and *Aurélia*.

162. ———. "Nerval et Ragotin." *Revue d'Histoire Littéraire de la France*, LI (1951), 480–82.

Comments on the general influence on Nerval of Scarron's *Le Roman comique* and, in particular, on the figure of Ragotin, the rejected lover of L'Etoile whose desire to kill himself may have had some bearing on Gérard's suicide.

163. Gsteiger, Manfred. *Literatur des Ubergangs.* Bern: Francke Verlag, 1963. 173p.

A short chapter on the sonnet "Myrtho" is included on pp. 31–35.

164. Guédenet, Pierre. "Note sur la collaboration de Théophile Gautier au *Monde Dramatique* de Nerval en 1835." *Romance Notes*, I, no. 2 (1960), 113–16.

Discusses primarily the importance of Gautier's contributions to the *Monde Dramatique* and includes very little on Nerval. The author might have suggested the possible reaction of Nerval to those articles by Gautier which were ultimately to make up Chapter XI of *Mademoiselle de Maupin*, a work that undoubtedly influenced Gérard. (cf. 260)

165. Guichard, Léon. *La Musique et les lettres au temps de romantisme.* Paris: Presses Universitaires de France, 1955. 424p. [Université de Grenoble. Publications de la Faculté des Lettres.]

The author devotes a complete chapter (pp. 330–54) in Part III of this monumental study to Gérard de Nerval and his role in the development of music in France. Unlike Coeuroy (84) and Tiersot (370), Guichard takes into consideration and comments on all of Gérard's musical activity: his part in the development of the French *chanson populaire*, his musical criticism, his participation as a librettist in the operatic theatre, etc. Although Gérard much preferred the *chanson* and musical romance to serious music, he nevertheless demonstrated an excellent knowledge of opera and a full appreciation of most experimental music of the day. As coauthor of *Piquillo* and *Les Monténégrins*, he was closely associated with Monpou and Limnander, while his other musical interests helped to bring about close friendships with Meyerbeer, Berlioz, Wagner, and especially Liszt. Guichard classifies Nerval's libretti as mediocre, and with regard to most of Gérard's musical essays, he states: "Ce sont là des remarques de critique dramatique, d'homme de théâtre et de librettiste, plutôt que de musicien" (p. 346). His general conclusion is that Gérard can hardly be considered a talented librettist or music critic and that "dans le domaine musical . . . son meilleur titre . . . est d'avoir ramené l'attention des lettrés, ses lecteurs, sur le trésor, alors si peu connu, de nos chansons populaires" (p. 350).
  a. C. M. Girdle-Stone. *French Studies*, X, no. 4 (1956), 363–64.
  b. L. Thompson. *Kentucky Foreign Language Quarterly*, IV (1957), 164–69.

166. *Guide Littéraire de la France.* Paris: Hachette, 1964. 836p. ["Bibliothèque des Guides Bleus."]

Thirty-three entries geographically locate Nerval in Paris and in the various provincial centers.

167. Guilbert, Charles. *L'Envers du génie.* Paris: Albin Michel, 1927. 251p.

Dr. Guilbert's first essay (pp. 27–71) is on Gérard de Nerval and represents little more than a clinical approach to the poet. The attempt here is aimed at analyzing Gérard's hallucinations (or dream states) as depicted in *Aurélia* and not at studying the artistic aspects of the work which show his genius.

168. Guillaume, Jean. *Les Chimères de Nerval. Edition critique.* Bruxelles: Palais des Académies, 1966. 171p.

This critical edition contains a number of new observations on the sonnets (showing, for example, that no modern edition reproduces faithfully the authoritative text of 1854), but is so poorly organized and so weighed down with superfluous documentation it is practically impossible to use. The most scrupulous consideration is given to previous editions and to the various manuscripts, allowing the author to develop eventually a chronological relationship between Nerval's letter "Trois jours de Folie," Dumas' presentation of "El Desdichado," the Eluard and Lombard manuscripts, and the text of 1854. Photocopies of the documents are included under separate fold at the end of the book.

169. ———. "Sur un tercet d' 'Artémis.' " *Etudes Classiques*, XXXI, no. 1 (1963), 34–41.

An attempt to trace and isolate the sources of imagery in the first tercet of the sonnet. The following suggestions are made: "Sainte napolitaine" is Saint Lucia, a name that expresses the idea of light; "aux mains pleines de feux" refers also to Lucia of Syracuse, who ripped out her eyes, carrying them in her hands, to preserve her virginity; "Rose au coeur violet" is linked with fire symbolism; "fleur de Sainte Gudule" involves the symbolic lily and the lighted lamp of the virgin Gudule; "As-tu trouvé ta Croix" suggests again Saint Gudule and the constellation of the Swan, usually designated by the Southern Cross; "dans le désert des cieux" is best explained by an analogy with "Non, Dieu n'existe pas!" of "Le Christ aux Oliviers." The note concludes with further comments on the inscription D.M.-LUCIUS. AGATHO. PRISCUS, which essentially signifies the masculine form of the three virgins, Lucia, Agatha, Prisca.

170. Guyon, Robert. "Comme une suite à un ajour d'Arcane 17." *La Brèche*, no. 6 (1964), 78–87.

Attempts to explain the enigmatic comments ("Cigne allemand," "feu G-rare," "Je suis l'autre") inscribed on the portrait of Nerval reproduced in Jean Richer's *Gérard de Nerval et les doctrines ésotériques* (303). The author points out a type of Egyptian statuary known as "à la nageuse" and suggests that Nerval discovered "le principe même qui conditionnait la métamorphose essentielle de ces cuillers à fard dites 'à la nageuse,' et il l'a fixé en marge de son portrait de 1854." An intensive investigation of Arcana 17 of the Tarot leads Guyon to relate certain of its aspects with the symbolism of Egyptian art and, in turn, with Gérard's concept of the *double* in *Voyage en Orient*.

171. Haedens, Kléber. *Gérard de Nerval, ou la sagesse romantique.* Paris: Bernard Grasset, 1939. 159p.

One of the first biographies to attempt to distinguish Nerval's "romanticism" from that of his contemporaries and to place the poet in his proper poetic inheritance. As opposed to the other Romantics of the period, who sought to create by exposing the surface of their hearts, "pour Nerval créer, c'est remonter aux sources de l'existence, c'est porter le faisceau de lumière au sein de la plus douce nuit" (p. 55). These efforts on Gérard's part to transcend worldly existence in the work of art and in his everyday life place him on a pedestal above his fellow writers.

172. Hassan El Nouty. "Le Calife Hakem et Gérard de Nerval." *Revue du Caire*, XXI (1958), 191–95.

Demonstrates first the exactness of Nerval's historical facts and descriptions in the *Histoire du Calife Hakem*, and second the means by which the poet utilized historical Oriental background to create the personal myth. "Gérard de Nerval appartient à cette lignée d'auteurs pour qui l'Orient demeure le dépositaire du savoir secret et redoutable, et dont l'exotisme ne découle pas de la manie du pittoresque mais du désir incoercible de sonder la vérité cachée des choses."

173. ———. *Le Proche-Orient dans la littérature française de Nerval à Barrès*. Paris: Nizet, 1958. 338p.

The first chapter of this superb study deals with the pre-eminence of the Egyptian theme in Nerval's *Voyage en Orient*, which, according to El Nouty, is not only the most interesting piece of Romantic travel literature but also the first work of its type to approach the subject in a completely artistic fashion. As the author observes, "Avant elle [*Voyage en Orient*], les relations de voyage en Orient étaient hybrides, tributaires d'autres genres" (p. 25). With Nerval, travel literature becomes a specifically defined artistic genre, the most refined expression of which will occur in the work of Pierre Loti. Unlike his fellow Romantic travelers, Gérard sought and found in the East (and particularly in Egypt) more than an exotic vision: "Il a établi une zone neutre entre l'exotisme des Romantiques et celui des époques postérieures dont le héraut sera Gustave Flaubert" (p. 26). Included in Chapter III of the study is an analysis of Gérard's artistic originality in the *Histoire de la Reine du Matin* and the *Histoire du Kalife Hakem*.

a. F. J. Warne. *French Studies*, XVII, no. 1 (1963), 92–93.

174. Hefke, George W. "Gérard de Nerval and Karl Gutzkow in March 1842." *Revue de Littérature Comparée*, XXXIV (1960), 451–55.

In the hope of accounting in part for Nerval's activities during "cette funèbre année 1842," the author brings to light a letter written on March 27, 1842, by the German writer Karl Gutzkow while he was in Paris. This brief document related the possibility of Nerval's becoming a "research assistant" for the Odéon, whereby the poet would have gathered German sources for new French plays to be performed at the theatre. If Gérard accepted the offer of his friend. Auguste Lireux (director of the Odéon), the project was short-lived because of the preparations necessary for the trip to the East in December, 1842. Gutzkow's letter not only furnishes further information on the poet's daily activity during this year, but "[it also] supplies us with further proof of Nerval's inclination and talents as a *germaniste*."

175. Henriot, Emile. "Une Explication des *Chimères*." *Le Temps* (10 janv. 1939), 3.

A review of 244, with no additional observations.

176. Huber, Egon. "Gérard de Nervals Meisternovelle *Sylvie*." *Deutschland-Frankreich*, II (1957), 169–75.

This astute commentary analyzes in detail both the rich inner symmetry of *Sylvie* and the actual creative means by which Nerval, always demonstrating a high consciousness of art, formulated his fiction. In discussion of the *nouvelle*'s intricate architecture the author distinguishes the three major love cycles (Adrienne-Sylvie-Aurélia) and shows how each adheres to three great curves that, at times, are almost bilaterally symmetrical with the central mid-point (Chapters VI and VII) of the story. To further emphasize Nerval's obsessive desire for perfect balance, Huber also notes certain themes and images that the poet develops in strict accordance with the general numerical structure.

177. Huige, Frida F. L. "Nerval's *Aurélia*: Schizophrenia and Art." *American Imago*, XXII, no. 4 (1965), 255–74.

Still another effort to study Nerval and his work according to Freudian principles. An attentive reading of the poet's correspondence and *Aurélia* shows him suffering from "chronic undifferentiated schizophrenia." The author concludes (rather questionably!): "Nerval surmounted his difficulties and transformed them into a 'healthy' work of art."

178. Humphrey, George. "Gérard de Nerval ou le retour à l'innocence." *Le Bayou*, XXIV, nos. 81–82 (1960), 29–35.

Introductory comments on Nerval's metaphysical relationship with Baudelaire, Apollinaire, Proust, and the Surrealists lead the critic to a lucid interpretation of Gérard's poetic method. In his effort to transcend reality, Nerval found in the illuminist tradition a means by which to resolve the enigmas of love and of life, a method that allowed him to "understand" again the purity of childhood by means of the dream. "Toute la psychologie de Nerval est orientée vers le passé, vers l'origine. Sa descente est un retour à la pureté." By dream the poet accomplishes a synthesis of time, whereby all terrestrial conflicts take on the aspect of continuity: "Par le rêve il se place en dehors du temps et n'entrevoit plus l'éternité ou la mort comme une suite à la vie. L'éternité et le temps se confondent dans les songes."

179. Irisawa, Yasua. "Sur *l'Octavie* de Nerval." *Bulletin de la Société de Littérature Française* (1960), 90–98. [Résumé in French, pp. 184–86.]

Interprets Octavie as a figure of carnal love and perhaps a figure of "érotisme déchaîné."

180. Jean, Raymond. "Le Centenaire de *Sylvie* ou Gérard de Nerval réaliste." *Lettres Françaises*, 480 (1953), 3.

Interesting observations on *Sylvie* "une oeuvre littéraire dense, précise, consciente." The profundity of the *récit* resides in its revelation of time, which is presented on three different levels: "jadis," "naguère," and "aujourd'hui."

181. ———. "De Nerval et quelques humoristes anglais." *Revue de Littérature Comparée*, XXIX (1955), 94–104.

Nerval knew and demonstrated an admirable knowledge of certain English authors, especially the eighteenth-century humorists. While the dialectic style of *Angélique* suggests the obvious influence of Sterne — whose prose techniques Gérard may have learned from a reading of Diderot's *Jacques le fataliste* — Swift (*Gulliver's Travels*) and Dickens (*Sketches by Boz*) undoubtedly had some influence on Gérard's *Voyage en Orient* and *Nuits d'octobre*. Jean also sees certain similarities between *Sylvie* and *Promenades et souvenirs* and Lewis Carroll's *Alice in Wonderland*. (cf. 141)

182. ———. "Encore Nerval." *Cahiers du Sud*, XLV, no. 349 (1958), 446–49.

Argues that Nerval should be studied as a nonmystic, nonabstract writer, although the possibility of esoteric influences should not be overlooked. The author outlines the primary methods of approach that have been applied to Nerval's work (occultism, esotericism, spiritual symbolism, crypto-psychology, and literary psychoanalysis) and states that more attention should be placed on Gérard's artistic merits.

183. ———. "Gérard de Nerval et les visages de la Nature." *Mercure de France*, CCCXII, no. 1054 (1951), 248–58.

Although nature is important throughout Nerval's works, he cannot be considered a nature poet in the Romantic sense. Nature, which for the poet is "le cadre des premières réactions de la sensibilité," represented for Nerval an actual force that possessed his language, his personal alchemy. In accordance with Bachelard's systematic method, Jean discusses the presence of the four elements of nature in Nerval's work: "Feu," "Terre," "Air," and "Eau."

184. ———. *Nerval par lui-même*. Paris: Editions du Seuil, 1964. 190p. [Coll. "Ecrivains de toujours," no. 68.]

A fresh and original approach to the poet that will be appreciated particularly by the nonspecialist. While the first chapter offers a chronological discussion of the major critical studies on Nerval and the second a short, clear, and concise biography, the remainder of the book is devoted to the art of Nerval. In his completely original and well-organized analyses of *Sylvie*, *Aurélia*, and the *Chimères*, the author demonstrates what is perhaps a unique appreciation of the poet and his art. Probing comments on the close relationship of Proust and Nerval are especially valuable. The 75 illustrations scattered through the book are well chosen and fascinating, and the representative texts at the end demonstrate the very best of Nerval.

    a. *Bulletin Critique du Livre Français*, no. 229 (1965), 11.
    b. J. Kneller. *French Review*, XXXVIII, no. 6 (1965), 805–6.
    c. G. Raillard. *Le Français dans le Monde*, no. 30 (1965), 47–48.

185. ———. "Nerval romancier." *Cahiers du Sud*, XLII, no. 331 (1955), 390–404.

The best, most detailed study to date of Nerval's one novel, *Le Marquis de Fayolle*. A full account of the work's meaning and a complete résumé of the plot are followed by an intricate analysis of structure, characters, and major themes. Jean remarks significantly that this unfinished work must be considered in two different lights: first as a *feuilleton* that was read and discarded by readers of *Le Temps*, and second as an artistic *récit* that demonstrates in other areas Nerval's talent as a prose writer. The novel is rich in symbolism, and of particular interest is the dominant father-son relationship: "Au fond là est l'essentiel du roman: le conflit survenu entre un père et un fils qui ne

se connaissent pas et que des circonstances historiques opposent avec vio-
lence." In what appears to be the poet's most objective work, we decipher the
most personal allusions to his own existence. Episodes of the novel are
linked with aspects of *Sylvie* and *Promenades et souvenirs*, and the author
concludes that, although one would not normally seek out Nerval's message
in a dry historical *feuilleton, Le Marquis de Fayolle* may very possibly shed
considerable light on numerous aspects of the poet's major work.

186. ———. "L'Oeil critique de Gérard de Nerval." *Lettres Françaises*, no. 825
      (19–25 mai 1960), 2.

Emphasizes the importance of Nerval's journalistic career, which enabled
him to grasp better "ce sens de l'actuel élargi jusqu'à l'universel." To understand fully the poet's use of syncretism, his love of archetypes, and his obsession with the theatre, one must view Nerval as his contemporaries saw him,
"un homme de culture, un merveilleux *liseur*," a man who was forced by profession to constantly demonstrate an "oeil critique."

187. ———. "Rousseau selon Nerval." *Europe*, 391–92 (1961), 198–205.

Jean-Jacques Rousseau confirmed for Gérard the idea that an author could
consider himself the essential subject of his own work. It was Rousseau's
"miroir" that fascinated Nerval and that affected his creation of the personal
myth. Gérard's "culte des lieux," so essential in the development of his mythology, is greatly influenced by his memory of Rousseau's "pays." Rousseau
becomes for Nerval a spiritual intercessor, "un frère intemporel dont Nerval
recherche le patronage." (cf. 196)

188. ———. "Le Vert Paradis de Gérard." *Cahiers du Sud*, XXVIII, no. 292
      (1948), 413–18.

A sensitive study of "le vert paradis des amours enfantines" evoked in Nerval's
Promenades et souvenirs, the substance of which offers the key to Gérard's
personal myth. This "vert paradis," animated by the figures of Fanchette,
Célénie, and Héloïse, resembles that of Baudelaire in that the evocation of a
definite past act serves to create an image. However, whereas Baudelaire's
green paradise was a lost region, Gérard's is a Proustian recaptured paradise
that gives depth to the poetic creation.

189. John, Alfred. *Gérard de Nervals Beziehungen zum Orient.* Greifswald:
      E. Hartmann, 1912. 103p.

The first foreign doctoral thesis to appear on Nerval, this early study is also
the first to consider the *Voyage en Orient* as something more than a secondary
work. After stating that many of Gérard's mystical ideas had been formed
before he left for the East, the author closely investigates numerous sources
that might have initially influenced the poet and his work.

190. Jourda, Pierre. "Les Souvenirs sont cors de chasse." *Revue des Sciences
      Humaines*, Fasc. 91 (1958), 417–18.

Points out Nerval's use of "le cor" as connected with the theme of "le souvenir" in *Sylvie* (Chap. I) and in the *Dernier Feuillet.* Jourda cites these
references as the source of Apollinaire's line in the *Alcools*.

191. Juden, Brian. "Nerval héros mythique." *Mercure de France*, CCXII, no. 1054 (1951), 259–66.

Pointing out the close personal relationship between Nerval and the heroic Faust, the author discusses the various means by which Gérard was able to create his own heroic personality. The act of identifying himself with his genealogical past allowed the poet to develop his own personal hero within the dream world: ". . . la race, cette série d'existences dont il fallait remonter la chaîne, afin de voyager librement dans le temps."

192. Kanters, Robert. "Sur une gravure imaginaire de Meryon." *Tour Saint-Jacques*, 13–14 (1958), 5–7.

That Meryon never produced an engraving of the Tour Saint-Jacques would not imply that his concept of the great city and his work were not of the same nature as that of Nerval: "Il y a, et chez Nerval et chez Meryon, un sens très vif de . . . la réalité fantastique." The universe described in *Aurélia* recalls the general haunting atmosphere of a Meryon, "[laquelle] seule peut minutieusement reconstituer à la fois l'aspect de la pierre et le sens du monument, l'aspect du ciel et le sens des signes qui y sont inscrits."

193. Kiès, A. "Une source d' 'El Desdichado': *Le Diable boiteux* de Lesage." *Lettres Romanes*, VII (1953), 357–58.

This critic finds the source of Nerval's title in Lesage's *Le Diable boiteux*, in the chapter entitled "Des foux enfermés," which tells of a certain Don Blaz Desdichado. Due to the death of his wife, Don Blaz becomes insane. However, his insanity was perhaps due to the fact that "il a été obligé de rendre aux parents de la défunte cinquante mille ducats qu'il avait reçus d'elle [son épouse]." Kiès suggests that Nerval might possibly have read the story at Dr. Blanche's asylum.

194. Kneller, John W. "An Approach to *Aurélia*," in *Aurélia ou le rêve et la vie* (édition critique de Jean Richer). Paris: Minard, 1965, pp. 334–39. [Résumé in French, p. 340.]

Maintains that the *expérience* of *Aurélia* should be viewed as a poetic, psychological, and religious experiment, whereby the poet both creates and elaborates the personal myth.

195. ———. "*Aurélia* across the Channel and the Atlantic," in *Aurélia ou le rêve et la vie* (édition critique de Jean Richer). Paris: Minard, 1965, pp. 341–47.

Traces in some detail Nerval's (and not *Aurélia*'s) gradual popularity in England and the United States, emphasizing the influential role that Arthur Symons' *The Symbolist Movement in Literature* (1899) played in the development. The author includes in his discussion such names as Andrew Lang, T. S. Eliot, Richard Aldington, Peter Quennell, S. A. Rhodes, Alison Fairlie, and Norma Rinsler, concluding that "[Nerval] has come to occupy in the British Isles and the United States a position of first importance among the poets of France."

196. ———. "Nerval and Rousseau." *PMLA*, LXVIII (1953), 150–69.

An astute, well-organized study of the Romanticism of Nerval and Rousseau and of the extent to which Nerval was indebted to Rousseau for inspiration. Pointing out initially that Gérard admired Jean-Jacques as an artist rather than as a thinker, Kneller demonstrates to what degree *La Nouvelle Héloïse*, the *Confessions*, the *Rêveries du promeneur solitaire*, and the *Consolations des misères de ma vie* had a special meaning for Nerval. He draws significant parallels between the *Nouvelle Héloïse* and Gérard's *Roman à faire* and *Le Marquis de Fayolle*, between Rousseau's *Confessions* and Nerval's *Angélique*; and he notes how Gérard, in the realm of dream literature, profited from and went far beyond Rousseau's "affirmation of the subconscious self as a separate state to be found by cultivating the faculty of inner mediation." Like Rousseau, Nerval felt the old alliance between music and poetry, and his knowledge of Rousseau's *Consolations des misères de ma vie* and the *Devin du village* most probably helped to stimulate his interest in popular song and folk tradition. Kneller notes further that after 1853 Gérard abandoned Jean-Jacques Rousseau and his own effort to recapture the spirit of his Valois soil, only to fulfill his genius in the form of *Aurélia*. (cf. 187)

197. ———. "The Poet and his Moira: 'El Desdichado.' " *PMLA*, LXXV (1960), 402–9.

One of the most plausible explications of the sonnet. The poem is seen primarily as the revelation of a man's poetical experience compressed into a few words, and not a distribution of various clues to events in the poet's life. Of special importance is the author's observation that the Spanish "Desdichado" does not mean "disinherited" ("deseredado"), but rather "unfortunate." Kneller acknowledges the possible hermetic sources of terms in the poem, but insists that such sources do not provide the essential meaning. He approaches the poem not as an enigmatic work "in which hieroglyphic figures are used to conceal its true meaning from all but the initiate," but as a work complete in itself. It is the story of the "hero-poet, who, like Orpheus, has through a transgression brought about the death of his loved one, and who . . . has transformed his experience into poetry."

198. Lacôte, René, and Madelaine Ozeray. *Le Rêve et la vie de Gérard de Nerval.* Paris: Seghers, 1958.

See 255.

199. Lacretelle, Jacques de. "La Galerie des amants. I: De Voltaire à Stendhal; II: De Keats à d'Annunzio." *Revue des Deux Mondes* (1 août 1963), 334–45; (15 août 1963), 492–506.

Includes portrait of and material on Nerval as lover.

200. Lalou, René. *Vers une alchimie lyrique. De Sainte-Beuve à Baudelaire.* Paris: Librairie Crès, 1927. 267p.

Classifying Nerval as "assurément parmi les initiateurs de l'alchimie poétique" (p. 48), this early study demonstrates a remarkable perception in relation to the poet and his art. Although the section on Gérard (pp. 48–65) is generally of a biographical nature, Lalou does attempt to define Nerval's

Romanticism as "une conception très précise" (p. 53), and he pays adequate attention to the poet's Germanism (pp. 54–58). He furthermore interprets the sonnets "El Desdichado" and "Artémis" as "poèmes où l'alchimiste a réussi ce miracle de prêter à ses deux hallucinations d'une descente aux enfers et de fiançailles avec une morte immortelle la dense suggestion des incorruptibles vérités" (p. 65).

201. Larroutis, M. "Une Enigme nervalienne: 'Erythréa.'" *Revue d'Histoire Littéraire de la France*, LIX, no. 3 (1959), 365–73.

Designating the Erythrean Sea (which, according to one source, was the same for the Greeks as the Red Sea and the Indian Ocean) as the object signified in the title of the sonnet, and discussing the alchemical sources of certain images, the author states that the poem is a prayer to the feminine divinity in her multiple forms. However complex the sonnet may be, it demonstrates a profound unity, which it owes "au thème de la déesse mère, de 'la primitive Isis, au voile éternel, au masque changeant,' du 'féminin céleste,' que le poète veut retrouver dans toutes les mythologies et dans toutes les religions."

202. Laurant, M. "Explication française: Gérard de Nerval à Ermenonville." *Ecole* (31 mars 1962).

Explication de texte of *Sylvie*, Chapter IX.

203. Lebois, André. "Exégèse des *Chimères*." *Le Bayou*, XIII, no. 69 (1957), 317–34.

See 205.

204. ———. "Exégèse des *Chimères*." *Revue de la Méditerranée*, XVII (1957), 521–46.

See 205.

205. ———. *Vers une élucidation des Chimères de Nerval*. Paris: Minard, 1965 [Archives des Lettres Modernes; Archives Nervaliennes, 1]. 32p. [Also published as "Exégèse des *Chimères*," in *Le Bayou*, XIII, no. 69 (1957), 317–34, and in *Revue de la Méditerranée*, XVII (1957), 521–46.]

Stating that "les *Chimères* ne sont pas poésie pure," Lebois analyzes each sonnet (except those which form "Le Christ aux Oliviers," which he curiously leaves out) in terms of myth and the poet's personal experiences. He views the sonnets as poetry that can be appreciated and understood "sans faire intervenir le tarot ni la kaballe" (p. 29).

206. Le Bot, Marc. "Gérard de Nerval." *Europe*, no. 353 (1958), 3–9.

Likens the world of Nerval to that portrayed in Corot's "Souvenir de Morte-fontaine," a poetic world made up, not of Romantic flamboyance and artificiality, but of permanence and the desire to reconcile the human soul with truth. Nerval's thought is that of the eighteenth-century mystics and occultists. Whereas the other Romantics attempted to imitate human symbolic types, Gérard tried to regulate his own destiny in terms of universal images and figures, thus becoming the agent of his own fate. The lyricism of the Romantics was a "littérature de confession," uncontrolled and lacking depth. Nerval adhered more to a "démarche volontaire, consciente, qu'il veut donner à un esprit et à l'inverse du mouvement d'abandon, de l'abdication de l'homme devant les Puissances qu'on découvre au sein de la nuit du non-savoir." The Romantics attempted to create the work of art by imitating the pathos of their existence; Gérard created his work of art by first creating his life.

207. Le Breton, George. "L'Alchimie dans *Aurélia*: 'Les Mémorables.'" *Fontaine*, no. 45 (1945), 687–706.

An extremely rich and valuable study. While the first part of the article points out Dom Pernety's *Fables égyptiennes et grecques* and *Dictionnaire mytho-hermétique* as the sources for Nerval's "Mémorables" (pp. 687–99), the second part, "La Création poétique chez Nerval," discusses clearly the means by which and the reason why Gérard was attracted to esoteric and particularly alchemical texts: "Le poète a vu dans l'opération alchimique conçue comme une suite d'allégories, non la transmutation d'une matière, mais celle d'une imagination et il a donné à cette symbolique non la valeur d'un simple artifice de création littéraire, mais la valeur d'un exercice de transfiguration intérieure." Like Novalis, Rimbaud, and A. Artaud, Nerval adhered to the great alchemical "théâtre des couleurs." "El Desdichado," "Artémis," "Myrtho," "Erythréa," and particularly "Horus" are like "des voyages à travers les couleurs." In Pernety's works Gérard recognized his own image; in alchemical and hermetic allegories he found "le passage d'une intériorité déchue à une intériorité glorieuse, d'images déprimantes à des images exaltantes, du soleil noir au soleil d'or."

208. ———. "La Clé des *Chimères*: l'alchimie." *Fontaine*, no. 44 (1945), 441–60.

Classifying "El Desdichado" as a "Soleil des sages," the author explicates each line of the sonnet in terms of alchemy and the Tarot. He demonstrates in minute detail how Nerval drew heavily from both Court de Gebelin's *Monde primitif, analysé et comparé avec le monde moderne . . .* and Dom Pernety's *Fables égyptiennes et grecques dévoilées* and *Dictionnaire mytho-hermétique*. The sonnet, likened to the alchemical Opus, passes through the various stages of putrefaction. The first part adheres to the alchemical *"noirceur,"* "la vrai signe d'une parfaite solution," while the second strophe represents the volatile and varicolored stage of the process: "Ce Phéréphata philosophique mis dans le vase avec sa mère pour fixer l'Elixir, se volatilise et produit différentes couleurs. . . ." The tercets signify the gradual recognition of the Philosopher's Stone and the ascension towards the White: "L'alchimiste a fait sortir le blanc du noir, c'est-à-dire que la sainte et la fée ont franchi l'Achéron et sont sorties de 'la putréfaction . . . ou la couleur noire, qui est le triste séjour de Pluton.'"

209. ———. "Le Pythagorisme de Nerval et la source des 'Vers dorés.'" *Tour Saint-Jacques*, 13–14 (1958), 79–87.

This article does more than point out Delisle de Sales' "Douze surprises de Pythagore" (from *De la philosophie de la nature*) as Nerval's source for the sonnet "Vers dorés." Le Breton discusses in detail Delisle's Pythagorean concept of nature and demonstrates how Nerval, in the sonnet and in *Les Illuminés*, adapted the eighteenth-century philosopher's pantheistic ideas to form a modern Pythagoreanism. He notes that Gérard found the title of his sonnet (originally "Pensée antique") in a section of Delisle's work entitled "Fragments des vers dorés de Pythagore" and that the poet's pantheistic doctrine adheres basically to the Pythagorean scale of the philosopher: ". . . d'abord l'intelligence des animaux, ensuite l'âme des plantes, enfin la sensibilité des pierres."

210. Le Breton, Jacques. "La Maison de santé du Dr. Blanche, ses médicins, ses malades." *Archives Médico-Chirurgicales de Normandi* (déc. 1963).

Includes a discussion on "Maladie et foi de Nerval."

211. Lecomte-Bammons, Mary. "A Propos des *Chimères* de Gérard de Nerval." *Cahiers d'Analyses Textuelles*, no. 4 (1962), 16–28. [Previously published as "Analyse textuelle et explication littéraire," in *Revue des Langues Vivantes*, XVII (1951), 302–11.]

Using "El Desdichado" as the model by which to exemplify a specific method of "analyse textuelle," the author very generally discusses the sonnet as an example of "poésie pure." She argues that the historic and literary origins of the works and imagery are of little value in trying to appreciate the poet's message, that even the use of the same expression (for example, "soleil noir") in two or more different works by Nerval helps in no way to define that expression in a particular context. What must be observed in the poem is "les mots et l'infini de leur 'magie suggestive.' "

212. ———. "Analyse textuelle et explication littéraire." *Revue des Langues Vivantes*, XVII (1951), 302–11.

See 211.

213. Le Hir, Yves. "La Versification de Gérard de Nerval." *Lettres Romanes*, X (1956), 409–22.

The only major study devoted entirely to Nerval's poetic forms and versification. The article takes up such topics as meter, poetic harmony, lyric forms, etc., and full attention is given to Nerval's sonnet construction. While the poet is said to have preferred the *sizain*, he employed numerous verse forms and always leaned heavily on the major forms developed by the Pléiade. The author concludes: "[Gérard] a voulu surtout que son vers fût un chant, une harmonie jusqu'à l'obsession," and that the perpetual discord between the rhythmic phrase and the syntactical one always found resolution in the ultimate harmony of the poetic thought.

214. Lemaître, Henri. "Gérard deux fois romantique." *Nouvelles Littéraires* (29 mai 1958), 9.

One of the very few efforts to define the "romanticism" of Nerval. Generally classifying Gérard as "le plus *complet* — et peut-être le seul vraiment *complet* — de nos romantiques," the author emphasizes the fact that Nerval in no way isolated himself from the literary, artistic, or musical activity of his day and that he indulged with enthusiasm in the spirit of the time. That his genius allowed him to transcend in his work the general superficiality of

Romanticism should suggest in no way that Nerval was not a Romantic. In fact, "c'est bien la *perfection* de ce romantisme-là qu'il a voulu et su réaliser," and we witness this accomplishment in *Voyage en Orient*, an essential document in the history of French Romanticism. However, Gérard rose above his fellow writers in his ability to synthesize exoticism and dream, the *pittoresque* and mysticism, fantasy and sincerity, language and poetry. His "romanticism" is thus of a double nature. It is "entre les mirages du monde extérieur et les mystères du monde intérieur, entre les exaltations de la sensibilité superficielle et les révélations de la sensibilité profonde, entre les fantasmagories de l'imagination et les mythes authentiques de l'âme."

215. Lévy, Paul. "Les Romantiques français et la langue allemande." *Revue Germanique*, XXXIX (1938), 233–38.

An important study on Nerval's knowledge of the German language and his talent as a translator of German authors. While Gérard's youthful confidence in the language resulted in numerous mistakes in the 1828 translation of *Faust*, his 1848 translation of Heine's *Intermezzo* demonstrated an increased linguistic proficiency and precision. Nerval's admirable ability as a translator is attributed to his talents as a poet, particularly in the case of the Heine translations.

216. Luquet, G.-H. "Gérard de Nerval et la Franc-Maçonnerie." *Mercure de France*, CCCXXIV, no. 1101 (1955), 77–96.

The most complete investigation of Nerval's possible links with Freemasonry. The author contends that, although Gérard was undoubtedly familiar with such works as the *Recueil précieux de la Maçonnerie adonhiramite*, and although one is able to see certain authentic Masonic elements in the *Histoire de la Reine du Matin*, there is little reason to believe that Nerval actually participated in the cult.

217. Maione, Italo. *Due profili (Stendhal — G. de Nerval)*. Napoli: Libreria Scientifica Editrice, 1954. 277p.

One of the most enlightened short biographies of Nerval in Italian. Demonstrating a reasonably good knowledge of the best studies on the poet to appear up to 1954, the author includes in the introduction and conclusion interesting observations on "la visione di Nerval." For example: ". . . la sua inquietudine [quella di Nerval] si placava nell'abbandono alle visioni, nel contemplare, nel significato che afferrava delle *rêveries*, nell'espressione poetica in cui passavano subito i suoi sogni alleggerendo lo spirito, naturalmente, pianamente" (p. 272).

218. Malagié, M. "Note sur l'horoscope de Gérard de Nerval." *Tour Saint-Jacques*, 13–14 (1958), 27–31.

A rather artificial attempt to classify and explain certain events in Nerval's life in terms of the poet's horoscope. Rectifying the position of the horizon at 25° Scorpion (which would thus correspond in axes to 25° Taureau), Malagié establishes the position of Saturne-Mars, the fixed star, to which the poet was most closely linked.

219. Marek, Joseph-C. "La Source grecque et la source égyptienne dans la poésie de Nerval et d'Hölderlin." *Revue de l'Université Laval*, XII, no. 1 (1957), 3–16.

Demonstrates how "Nerval et Hölderlin sont réunis dans la mesure où ils constituent en leur plus grande pureté les figures symboliques de deux thèmes de pensée, l'un grec, l'autre égyptien, ou plutôt, au sein du thème grec, le départage de ce qui lui revient en propre et de ce qui est d'infiltration égyptienne." Whereas Hölderlin adhered in his poetry to the traditional concept of "la Grèce qui fournit au Classicisme français l'idée de l'équilibre humain," Nerval syncretized the Greek, Egyptian, Judaic, and Hindu worlds into a single and unique universe. Because of this, the many similar mythological symbols and images employed by the two Orphic poets take on completely different meanings. Marek demonstrates the case of Nerval by explicating the sources of the sonnets "Erythréa" ("A Mme Aguado") and "Delfica." In conclusion he notes: "Retour à la naissance de la civilisation, retour à l'origine du langage, tel est le caractère commun de [ces] deux poètes."

220. Marenzi, Maria L.-A. "La 'Parola' di Gérard de Nerval." *Annali della Facoltà di Lingue e Letterature Straniere di ca'Foscari*, II (1963), 9–26.

Stating her intention to "raccogliere ad uno ad uno i frantumi delle voci discordi e ricomporle nella voce e nel canto," the author proceeds in a rather awkward and superficial manner to divide Nerval's "parole" into five categories, which, in turn, she applies to the various texts of the poet. She leans too heavily on the studies of Poulet and Richard and, in truth, makes few original or profound observations.

   a. *Studi Francesi*, VIII, no. 1 (1964), 176.

221. Marie, Aristide. *Bibliographie des oeuvres de Gérard de Nerval*. Paris: Librairie Ancienne Edouard Champion, 1926. 281p.

Represents the first attempt to establish formally a listing of Nerval's works and critical studies on the poet. The bibliography contains 345 references to primary works and 191 references to articles before 1926 devoted to Gérard de Nerval. There are a number of significant errors, such as certain "oeuvres de jeunesse" that are not by Nerval. The volume includes an entire chapter on "Pseudonymes et apocryphes," a short iconographical list, and a complete chronological index.

222. ———. *Gérard de Nerval, le poète et l'homme* (d'après des manuscrits et documents inédits). Paris: Hachette, 1914. 436p. [Reprinted in 1955.]

This monumental study of Gérard de Nerval, published during the early period when the poet was barely recognized, served as a basis for future critical interest and appreciation. It is the first documented biography of Nerval, including 24 plates, an incomplete bibliography, notes, reproductions of the "Acte de décès" and Nerval's "Note généalogique," and a genealogical table. The 1955 reprint does not include all the plates of the original edition or the bibliography. Still an invaluable tool for all serious research on Nerval.

   a. Y.-G. Le Dantec. *Education Nationale*, no. 7 (1955), 3–5.
   b. M. Lobet. *Revue Générale Belge* (1955), 1051–52.
   c. R. Ternois. *Education Nationale*, no. 8 (1956), 26.

223. Marie, Gisèle, and Madelaine Cavé. "Gérard aima-t-il Jenny Colon ou la comtesse d'Egmont?" *Nouvelles Littéraires* (29 mai 1958), 1, 10.

Brings to light François Ancelot's play, *Madame d'Egmont ou Sont-elles deux*, the play to which the poet refers in *Sylvie* and in which Jenny Colon held the leading role from April 25 to July 1, 1833. The feminine figure interpreted by Jenny recalled for the poet the Baronne de Feuchères, whom he idolized as a child at Mortefontaine and who later become fused with the heroine of Ancelot's play and the actress Jenny Colon. Furthermore, Marie believes that Gérard identified himself with the heroic Renaud of the play and later attempted to recreate the role in his own play, *Corilla*, "pièce qu'il destine à Jenny, une simple transposition de Madame d'Egmont."

224. Marix-Spire, Thérèse. *Les Romantiques et la musique. I.* Paris: Nouvelles Editions Latines, 1954. 710p. [Balzac, Stendhal, Musset, Lamartine, Gautier, Nerval, Maurice de Guérin.]

Includes comments on Nerval and his role in the development of the *chanson populaire*.
   a. *Revue Générale Belge* (1955), 1597–98.
   b. *Times Literary Supplement* (July 11, 1955), 362.

225. Massignon, Louis. "De l'essor de l'imagination musulmane, jusqu'en Chrétienté, à propos des rêves et des contes nervaliens." *Tour Saint-Jacques*, 13–14 (1958), 55–59.

Suggests that Nerval, "[qui] me paraît plus proche des Musulmans que des Spirits," adhered to a Moslem folkloric doctrine in his practice of Freemasonry and that this initiate of the "verbe mental" wanted to "islamiser son hétérodoxie chrétienne."

226. Maugis, Henri. "Gérard de Nerval: le poète." *Les Humanités*, 330 (1957), 20–24; 331 (1957), 22–27.

Stating that "les oeuvres poétiques de Gérard de Nerval peuvent être classées en deux catégories, sinon en trois," the author presents a well-prepared résumé of Nerval's poems. Part II of the essay includes a concise discussion of *Les Chimères* and the *Autres Chimères*, as well as an interesting commentary on the poet's use of the sonnet form. Further remarks on Gérard's "romanticism" demonstrate the author's sensitive understanding of the poet and his art.

227. ———. "Gérard de Nerval prosateur." *Les Humanités*, 325 (1957), 23–26; 326 (1957), 20–27.

Although the first of these two essays treats only biography, the résumé is concise and well done. The second essay concentrates on the major themes and on the style of *Voyage en Orient*, *Angélique*, *Sylvie*, and *Aurélia*.

228. Mauron, Charles. *Des métaphores obsédantes au mythe personnel. Introduction à la psycho-critique.* Paris: José Corti, 1963. 388p.

Chapter IV (pp. 64–80) is devoted to Nerval and expands on the author's theories expressed in 229. In Chapter IX (pp. 148–56), Mauron interprets myth in the sonnet "Artémis" in the light of his psychological theories.
   a. J. M. Cocking. *French Studies*, XIX, no. 1 (1965), 89–91.
   b. *Times Literary Supplement*, no. 3213 (Sept. 27, 1963), 741.

229. ———. "Nerval et la psycho-critique." *Cahiers du Sud*, XXXVI, no. 293 (1949), 76–97.

Justifiably questions Sébillotte's preconceived contention (348) that Nerval must be viewed in terms of his "échec sexuel." The possibility of sexual impotence can neither be confirmed nor disproved by a general reading of the poet's texts, for the works prove nothing with regard to Gérard's virility. Unlike Sébillotte, Mauron carefully examines the letters to Jenny Colon, *Aurélia, Les Chimères, Léo Burckart*, and numerous other pieces, in hopes of *objectively* defining the psychological trauma that so affected the poet's life and work. In accordance with certain essential "associations et symboles" (p. 92), the author studies such important factors as Nerval's reaction to his mother and father, the theme of the *double*, and the poet's formation of esoteric doctrines. Mauron's method of psychological analysis is effective and usually convincing, and, most admirable of all, his hypotheses are direct results of a close investigation of the texts.

230. Mériard, J. *De Corneille à Saint Denys Garneau*. Montréal, 1957.

Includes a discussion on "Le Mythe chez Nerval," pp. 91–108.

231. Mermier, Guy. "La Mort, la fatalité et l'amour dans le *Voyage en Orient*." *Le Bayou*, XVI, nos. 93–94 (1963), 359–63.

The author discusses certain episodes in *Voyage en Orient* in terms of Gérard's never-ending effort to dominate the omnipresent spectre of Death, to escape the hold of Destiny, and to abolish those elements which add to his "amour impossible."

232. Merz, Helen. *Traum und Wirklichkeit bei Gérard de Nerval*. Zurich: Leemann, 1929.

One of the first attempts to demonstrate the evolution of Nerval's thought in a world of fantasy and dream. Divided into three chapters, "Verdrängung," "Durchdringung," and "Auflösung," the thesis concentrates on six primary texts (the translation of *Faust, Le Voyage en Orient, Isis, Angélique, Octavie*, and *Aurélia*) and shows how they demonstrate the poet's gradual recession into the dream world. The work is generally a stylistic analysis, and little effort is made to study the substance of Nerval's creative art.

233. Meschonnic, Henri. "Essai sur la poétique de Nerval." *Europe*, 353 (1958), 10–33.

In this purely stylistic analysis, the author attempts to define Gérard's poetry in terms of its sounds, rhythms, and movements, not in terms of its imagery. He devotes the first part to Nerval's youthful imitative verse, emphasizing the influence of Ronsard and the Alexandrine and that of Corneille's dramatic technique in the composition of dramatic verse. While the treatment of the transition period between the early lyrics and the *Chimères* is quite superficial, discussions on the "Ballade populaire et la romance" and Nerval's skill with the sonnet form are quite acceptable. The author's definition of Nerval's technique in the sonnet is particularly interesting: "Il tend à isoler chaque strophe, et opposer aussi les trois derniers vers aux onze premiers par un changement de temps du verbe, déplaçant l'articulation de toute la pièce entre le premier et le second tercet. Une telle fragmentation rend un déchirement intérieur." The most valuable part of the study is the section entitled "La Composition des sonnets" (pp. 33–37), which is followed by a useful "Chronologie de la vie et des oeuvres."

234. Messiaen, Pierre. *Gérard de Nerval (Christianisme et occultisme)*. Paris: Morainville, 1945. 168p.

One of the most informative general studies on Nerval. Although the author does not pursue in detail his original topic, his résumé of the poet's life (pp. 9–75) and his astute commentaries on Gérard's major and minor works demonstrate his remarkable appreciation of the writer. Of particular interest are the chapters entitled "Lorely" and "Oeuvres d'intérêt secondaire," the latter of which includes plot summaries of *Le Marquis de Fayolle* and *Léo Burckart*. The final chapter, "L'Homme et l'artiste," portrays Nerval as one of the most influential figures of the Romantic period, as an admirable historian and journalist, and as a refined stylist: ". . . en tout ce qu'il a tenté et touché, il est au rang des plus grands" (p. 160).

235. Michaud, Guy. *Message poétique du symbolisme*. Paris: Nizet, 1951. 3 vols.

The author of this monumental study on the French Symbolist movement devoted two and a half pages (pp. 29–31) to Nerval's role in the development of the later movement. Gérard is spoken of as "le premier des aventuriers," the first poet to transcend reality and seek definition of his existence in the realm of symbol.

236. Milner, Max. *Le Diable dans la littérature française, de Cazotte à Baudelaire*. Paris: José Corti, 1960. 2 vols.

See Vol I, pp. 583–94, and Vol. II, pp. 274–309, for material related to Nerval.

237. Mondor, Henri. "Valéry a-t-il compris Nerval." *Nouvelles Littéraires* (29 mai 1958), 4.

Reviews Paul Valéry's judgment of Nerval, quoting his well-known opinion: "L'Oeuvre [de Nerval] est mince. Et il faut avouer que ce peu se réduit lui-même à une douzaine de strophes. Le reste est sans la moindre force. . . ." Although certain Nervalian elements can be traced in Valéry's work, the author doubts that the twentieth-century poet fully understood Gérard. (Cf. 374)

238. Montal, Robert. "Un Curieux Plagiat: *Piquillo*, opéra-comique d'Alexandre Dumas et Gérard de Nerval." *Le Thyrse* (1960), 406–13.

An excellent résumé of Nerval's theatre, its position in French dramatic tradition, and its importance in Gérard's literary career. The author notes that *Piquillo* ("ce facile libretto d'opérette [qui] n'est pas charme ni fantaisie"), written in collaboration with Dumas and the composer Monpou, was hailed by the critics as a new and original play. It is interesting that few realized the work virtually plagiarized the famous play *Le Chariot de terre cuite*, which Nerval also used for his dramatic version of *Le Chariot d'Enfant* in the *Monde Dramatique*. However, even though the general theme of the two plays is identical, Nerval's piece demonstrates better intrigue, more rapid dramatic action, and more sophisticated scenic effects. In conclusion, Montal points out that the subjects for all Nerval's plays (collaborations?), including

Léo Burckart, were drawn from other dramas (even by Molière!), and that, essentially, Gérard lacked creative imagination in the genre: "Sa part en effet reste toujours capitale dans la découverte des thèmes, et c'est pour leur organisation qu'il a jugé nécessaire de recourir à des spécialistes."

239. Moon, H. Kay. "Gérard de Nerval: A Reappraisal." *Brigham Young University Studies*, VII, no. 1 (1965), 40–52.

After rehashing the biography, the author "ventures a few observations regarding [Nerval's] short prose fiction" and attempts to determine Nerval's bearing in the twentieth century and his influence on modern French authors.

240. Moreau, Pierre. "A la suite des voyageurs français au Liban." *Revue des Sciences Humaines*, Fasc. 51–52 (1948), 222–35.

Includes Nerval among those Western travelers who found in the culture and religions of the East a means by which to transcend daily reality. The author emphasizes the fact that the events of Gérard's actual voyage barely correspond to the episodes he traces in the *Voyage en Orient*.

241. ———. *Amours romantiques*. Paris: Hachette, 1963. [Coll. "L'Amour et l'histoire."]

Nerval's amorous relationships are included in this "Carte de Tendre romantique."

242. ———. *Sylvie et ses soeurs nervaliennes*. Paris: Société d'édition d'enseignement supérieur, 1966. 99p.

On *Les Filles du Feu* and the artistic relationship between the stories that make up the collection. While Chapter I discusses in a brief chronological outline how the various parts of the work took shape, Chapter II is a study of dream and reality, love and dream, as portrayed in the stories. Also included in this chapter is an interesting analogy between *Octavie* and Mérimée's *Carmen*. Chapter III is a commentary on Nerval's abilities as a *conteur*.

243. Morgan, Estelle. "Bourgeois and Philistine." *Modern Language Review*, LVIII, no. 1 (1962), 69–72.

Traces the concept of the Philistine as the term is used in nineteenth-century literature, but simply mentions Nerval's statement, "Ohé! les bourgeois! les philistins damnés!"

244. Moulin, Jeanine. *Les Chimères. Exégèses*. Lille: Librairie Girard; Genève: Librairie Droz, 1949. 97p. [Published in 1937 as *Les Chimères de Gérard de Nerval*. Bruxelles: Cahiers du Journal des Poètes, no. 32.]

Preceded by a comprehensive general introduction of 46 pages, this line-by-line explication of the *Chimères* represents an admirable attempt to analyze formally the symbolic sense of each sonnet in hopes of demonstrating a general unity within the collection. Leaning heavily on Richer's esoteric theories and Le Breton's alchemical opinions, Moulin states that "les explications . . . ne constituent, en effet, que des points de repère qui permettent tout au plus de se diriger à travers les passages obscurs" (p. lii). Although her ideas are at times inconclusive and certain opinions rather nebulous, Moulin's study is extremely important as a single work devoted entirely to the elucidation of all the *Chimères*.

a. L. Guilloux. *Vendredi* (2 avril 1937).

b. E. Henriot. *Le Temps* (10 janv. 1939), 3.

c. J. Richer. "*Les Chimères* de G. de Nerval," *Paru* (mai 1948 et oct. 1949).

d. E. Souffrin. *French Studies*, IV, no. 4 (1950), 359–61.

245. ———. *Les Chimères de Gérard de Nerval*. Bruxelles: Cahiers du Journal des Poètes, no. 32, 1937. 99p.

See 244.

246. ———. "Gérard de Nerval et le mythe," *Bulletin de l'Académie Royale de Langue et de Littérature*, no. 3 (1957), 189–93.

Primarily a long, critical review of 121. After emphasizing Mme Durry's refusal to "enclore cette personalité multiforme dans une interprétation étriquée," the author suggests what she feels to be the essence of Nerval's problem, "sa terreur du néant": "S'il sonde le passé, le présent et l'avenir, s'il veut les unir et les confondre, c'est pour s'assurer de la permanence des choses, pour croire que son âme, que les âmes des êtres chers sont des *molécules* indestructibles, destinées à se rejoindre."

247. ———. "Gérard de Nerval, le ténébreux et l'inconsolé." *Revue Générale Belge*, XCI (1955), 823–33.

Retracing in part the major points of her 1949 exegetical study of the *Chimères* (244), the author suggests two qualities of Nerval's verse that make him unique as a Romantic poet: "l'atmosphère de l'irréel" and "sa mesure." Gérard's message was a brief one, and he felt this message could best be expressed in the sonnet, a form looked down upon by the other Romantics. Whereas "El Desdichado" evokes a poet's whole existence, "Delfica," "Artémis," and "Le Christ aux Oliviers" demonstrate the synthesis of his syncretic religious convictions. As a result, "le syncrétisme religieux du poète se complète par un syncrétisme amoureux." Admitting her failure to consider *Faust* while interpreting the sonnets, Moulin agrees here that "le poète a revécu, pas à pas, l'expérience de ce héros." Her general conclusion touches on an important topic: "Gérard de Nerval est le seul poète de sa génération qui ait vécu ses idéaux, le seul qui ait pris le romantisme au sérieux. Et il en est mort."

248. ———. "Langage de la poésie." *Les Annales*, 73e année, no. 192 (1966), 37–41.

Stating that "Gérard de Nerval fut le premier écrivain français à bouleverser les normes du langage poétique," the author remarks that Gérard thought his theatre would be the most durable part of his works. She adds: "Or, c'est dans *Les Chimères* et *Aurélia* que réside l'essentiel. C'est là qu'avant Rimbaud, les symbolistes et les surréalistes, il misa sur la magie du verbe plutôt que sur la logique et délivra le poème de la narration suivie."

249. Müller, Manfred. "Nervals Pandora-Fragment." *Zeitschrift fur französische Sprache und Literatur*, LXX, nos. 3–4 (1960), 139–48.

The first part of this article discusses Nerval's stay in Vienna in 1839; his encounter with Jenny Colon and Marie Pleyel in Brussels and with Marie

Pleyel in Vienna. Müller relates the Pandora fragment (*Voyage d'Italie. Panorama*) to *Sylvie*, and he suggests the following relationship: Jenny-Aurélia, Marie-Pandora. He cites furthermore a passage from *Faust* concerning earthly and spiritual love, which, in his opinion, would support the above relationship. The last part of his article is devoted to Nerval's language, which the author feels is of a rare purity.

> a. P. Cuireanu. *Studi Francesi*, V, no. 14 (1961), 371.

250. Nadal, Octave. "Poétique et poésie des Chimères." *Mercure de France*, CCCXXV (1955), 405–15.

Investigates the *Chimères* in terms of a major image: "la pierre animée par la lumière et par le verbe." The poetry is not so much the rhythmic and musical expression of ideas as it is the revelation of poetic experience by means of personal and mythical imagery. With this conviction in mind, the author discusses in detail qualities of the *Chimères* that separate this collection from the other lyric poetry of the time and that link Nerval's verse so closely with that of Baudelaire.

251. Nelson, Roy Jay. "L'Analyse visuelle de l'harmonie vocalique dans le vers français." *French Review*, XL, no. 3 (1966), 377–86.

Pp. 381–83 concern "El Desdichado."

252. [Nerval, Gérard de.] *Exposition organisée pour le centième de sa mort.* Paris: Bibliothèque Nationale, 1955. 98p.

An extremely fascinating and valuable catalogue that contains an annotated chronological listing of Nervaliana, including manuscripts, documents, editions, and eight photographic reproductions. Includes 380 items.

253. Noulet, E. *Etudes littéraires. L'hermétisme de la poésie moderne.* Mexico City: Talleras Graficos de la Editorial Cultura, 1944. 158p.

The sonnets "El Desdichado" and "Artémis" are the subjects of discussion on pp. 24–36.

254. Onimus, Jean. "Artémis ou le Ballet des Heures." *Mercure de France*, CCCXXIV, no. 1101 (1955), 73–76.

In this short commentary on the title of the sonnet "Artémis" ["Ballet des Heures"], the author attempts to explain the significance of the goddess' name in the light of the great Renaissance clock that Gérard mentions in *Sylvie*. "Diane accoudée sous le cadran, détachée de l'éternelle ronde des heures . . . devient pour [Nerval] le symbole même du Temps."

255. Ozeray, Madelaine, and René Lacôte. *Le Rêve et la vie de Gérard de Nerval.* Paris: Seghers, 1958.

No critical material. Includes a long dialogue by Ozeray entitled "Les Poireaux de Mortefontaine" (first published in *Les Lettres Françaises*, 22 mai 1958) and a short play entitled *Artémis* by Lacôte.

> a. A. Wurmser. *Lettres Françaises*, no. 753 (25–31 déc. 1958), 2.

256. Patry, André. "Gérard de Nerval." *Revue Dominicaine*, LX (1954), 231–41.

A rather uninteresting article that fails in its attempt to bring into focus the various oneiric, symbolic, and exotic elements of Nerval's *Filles du Feu, Voyage en Orient, Les Chimères*, and *Aurélia*.

257. Pellegrin, Jean. "Commentaire sur 'El Desdichado.'" *Cahiers du Sud*, LXI, nos. 387–388 (1966), 276–95.

Demonstrating throughout his comprehensive knowledge of Nerval scholarship (and attacking the superficial methods of many exegetes), the author, rather than offering any "new" interpretation of the sonnet, strives to show how "El Desdichado" is a magnificent, purely artistic statement of a man's desperate search for the absolute and his personal identity. Pellegrin's *explication de texte* is simple, sound, and well executed.

258. Petralia, F. "Note introduttive alla *Sylvie* di Nerval." *Lingue Estere*, no. 7 (1961), 1–14.

Taking into consideration the poet's psychological crises of 1852–1853, the author first comments (rather unconvincingly) on the chronological placement of scenes in *Sylvie*. The *nouvelle* is seen as containing little realism, for almost all the personages are transformed in the author's mind and in the work of art into an ideal arising out of "suggestioni lontane." *Sylvie* is the story of a child's paradise, transformed into the work of art by means of symbol and imagery.

    a. *Studi Francesi*, XVIX (1963), 177–78.

259. Peyre, Henri. *Literature and Sincerity*. New Haven: Yale University Press; Paris: Presses Universitaires de France, 1963. 362p. [Yale Romance Studies, Second Series, 9.]

Gérard de Nerval is included in a discussion of the Romantic novel and poetry. The author writes of Nerval's masterpiece: "*Aurélia* is a symbolic tale of rare beauty, but sincerity is hardly the word to apply to its mythical transformation of moods and events into a dream world" (p. 193).

260. Peyrouzet, Edouard. *Gérard de Nerval inconnu*. Paris: José Corti, 1965. 384p.

In this thorough, well-documented investigation of Nerval's genealogy, the author attempts to analyze multiple facets of the poet's work and existence in terms of his background and heredity. In order to reconcile the "mélange fortuit de Valois et de Gascogne, qui est à l'origine de l'instabilité de cette âme" (p. 9) and thus achieve a proper perspective of the "inconnu," Peyrouzet introduces many hitherto obscure personages who might have exercised a profound influence on Gérard. Of particular interest are the discussions on the "ingrate Sophie," the image of "la mère," the theme of *le double* as portrayed in *Le Calife Hakem* and *Léo Burckart*, and the shocking influence of Dr. Labrunie's doctoral thesis on his son.

    a. R.-M. Albérès. *Figaro Littéraire* (sept. 1965).

    b. J. Villas. *French Review*, XXXIX, no. 3 (1965), 459–60.

261. Pholien, Georges. "Lecture de Gérard de Nerval: 'El Desdichado.'" *Marche Romane*, VI (1956), 3–4.

A short analysis of the sonnet as a piece of poetic art complete within itself.

262. Pichois, Claude. "Le Chemin des Enfers s'ouvre entre deux piles de livres."
Nouvelles Littéraires (29 mai 1958), 8.

Although Gérard drew inspiration for *Les Filles du Feu* from his personal
experience, most of his ideas were the results of voracious reading. With the
possible exception of *Sylvie* ("une transposition poétique"), the collection
contains "borrowed" themes that the poet personalized and expounded. Mérimée's *Colomba* is cited as a typical example of this literary influence on
Nerval.

263. ⸻. "La Date du *Prince des Sots.*" *Revue d'Histoire Littéraire de la
France*, no. 2 (1964), 279–83.

Argues that Nerval's novel was written after 1836 and most probably after
1838.

264. ⸻. "Gérard traducteur de Jean-Paul." *Etudes Germaniques*, XVIII,
no. 1 (1963), 98–113.

Discusses and compares Nerval's 1830 translations of "Die Mondfinsternis"
("L'Eclipse de la lune") and "Die Neujahrsnacht eines Unglücklichen"
("La Nuit du Nouvel An d'un malheureux"), pointing out Gérard's changes
in linguistic detail and commenting on the poet's talent as a translator. It is
also suggested that another work, "Le Bonheur de la maison," always considered to be a translation from Jean-Paul, might well be by Nerval.

265. ⸻. *L'Image de Jean-Paul Richter dans les lettres françaises.* Paris: José
Corti, 1963. 526p.

Adequate attention is given to Nerval's knowledge of and debt to Jean-Paul,
whose work he translated and respected (cf. 264). In addition to his spiritual
attraction to the figure of Maria in Jean-Paul's works, Gérard, like many of
the Romantics, was fascinated by the German poet's cosmic vision of the
universe as expressed in the famous *Songe*. Studying the philosophic implications of the piece, Pichois notes how Gérard, unlike Vigny and Leconte de
Lisle, was able to borrow certain imagery and transform it into artistic and
original concepts. Comments on "Le Christ aux Oliviers" and the image of
the "Soleil noir" in this sonnet and other works are astute and stimulating.
See in particular pp. 276–87. (cf. 29)

266. ⸻. "Nerval et la Franc-Maçonnerie." *Le Monde* (27 août 1955).

Presentation of a letter discovered by the author, which might affirm Nerval's
participation in Freemasonry and which would negate the previous argument of G.-H. Luquet (216).

267. Pieltain, Paul. "Sur l'image d'un soleil noir." *Cahiers d'Analyse Textuelle*,
no. 5 (1963), 88–94.

An elaboration on the commentary by Gérald Antoine (6). Whereas Antoine
interpreted the black sun in terms of "la connaissance de l'écrivain (ou de sa
psychologie créatrice)," Pieltain is more concerned with an aesthetic analysis
of the image and the poetic context in which it is used. With regard to Nerval's

varied use of the black sun, Pieltain sees the one in "El Desdichado" as a "soleil éteint," whereas the one described in *Voyage en Orient* is a "soleil assombri qui enveloppe l'âme ainsi que la mélancolie."

268. Piron, Maurice. "La Composition de 'Delfica.'" *Studi Francesi*, VI, no. 16 (1962), 89–94.

Studies in reasonable detail the structure of the sonnet and its relationship with the sister sonnets "Myrtho" and "A J.-Y. Colonna." Unlike Nerval's other sonnets, these three demonstrate a clearly divided architecture, the subject of the first tercet of each in no way corresponding to that of the quatrains: ". . . dans l'un et l'autre cas, les quatrains et les tercets ne s'appellent pas plus qu'ils ne s'excluent." Since the interchangeable tercets best adhere in subject matter to the quatrains of "Delfica," Piron considers this sonnet in terms of its poetic movement, its imagery, and its sources in Virgil.
    a. *Lettres Romanes*, XIX, no. 3 (1965), 293.

269. Poirier, Jeanne. "Un Etrange Amoureux: Gérard de Nerval. Autour des *Lettres à Jenny Colon*." *La Table Ronde*, no. 96 (1955), 98–112.

The only critical study devoted exclusively to an interpretation of Nerval's letters to Jenny Colon. These letters, which manifest "une sincerité qui va au coeur" and which, contrary to the belief of many, were not written for posterity, represented for Gérard "une arme de conquête." Poirier discusses the various ideas concerning the poet's possible liaison with the actress, concluding that with such an unsolvable problem one must simply "lire ces lettres dans un esprit nervalien, croire avec Gérard que l'imagination est une source d'émotion plus forte que le réel."

270. Popa, Nicolas. "Les Sources allemandes de deux *Filles du Feu*." *Revue de Littérature Comparée*, X (1930) 486–520.

Shows *Jemmy* to be an imitation of the German Karl Postl's (Charles Sealsfield's) *Christophorus Bärenhauter im Amerikanerlande* and points out *Die Isis-Vesper* of Böttiger as the source of Nerval's article of 1845 entitled "Le Temple d'Isis, souvenirs de Pompei" and the later short story entitled *Isis*. The author concludes that, although Gérard imitated works by these two German authors, neither, it appears, exercised any veritable influence on him.

271. Porcher, Jean. "La Première Version d'*Aurélia*." *Nouvelles Littéraires* (18 janv. 1962), 1, 7.

Presentation of what is probably the original version of *Aurélia*, donated to the Bibliothèque Nationale by Mme Lucien-Graux. This text offers more concrete autobiographical facts: precise place names, names of personages, detailed information concerning the poet's stay in Brussels in 1840, etc. Adequate notes accompany the presentation.

272. Poulet, Georges. *Etudes sur le temps humain*. Paris: Plon, 1950. 407p.

Contains significant observations on Nerval and his poetic treatment of time. Of particular interest is Chapter XIV, which comments on the importance of Nerval's preface to his translation of the *Second Faust*.

273. ———. *Les Métamorphoses du cercle.* Paris: Plon, 1961. 304p.

Pages 244–68 are a reprint of 274.
   a. M.L.A. Marenzi. *Annali della Facoltà di Lingue e Letterature Straniere,*
      II (1963), 172–75.
   b. L. Normanno. *Culture Française,* XI, no. 1 (1964).

274. ———. "Nerval et le cercle onirique." *Cahiers du Sud,* XLII, no. 331 (1955),
347–63. [Reprinted in 273, pp. 244–68.]

Demonstrates how Nerval's mental anguish was constantly nourished by his
obsession with the image of the eternal circle. Dividing the study into three
sections, the author considers "Artémis" ("Ballet des Heures") as a point of
departure and shows how the poet attempted to create in the midst of the
circular dance of time a single, definable hour, an eternal moment, yet an
hour "composée de toutes." He draws attention to the image of the clock in
Voyage en Orient, Sylvie, Aurélia, and Goethe's *Faust,* an image which signifies that past world which is forever being rejuvenated, turning, wound up,
revolving around "la minute éternelle" of existence. Since all images revolve
with each other in the great circle of time and space, and since no image has
a totally individual nature, the symbolic oneiric circle must never be decom-
posed: "Faire qu'une nouvelle image ou un nouvel amour vienne se dessiner
sur la trame variée des autres; faire que 'les variations se succèdent à l'infini.' "

275. ———. "*Sylvie* ou la pensée de Nerval." *Cahiers du Sud,* XXV, no. 209
(1938), 665–708.

A monumental study of *Sylvie,* devoted primarily to the theme of time and the
various levels of reality in the short story on which the theme is constructed.
While the idyl demonstrates further the concept of "le mal romantique," the
poet's intuitive method of composition anticipates the art of Marcel Proust.
(cf. 276)

276. ———. *Trois essais de mythologie romantique.* Paris: José Corti, 1966. 183p.

While the first chapter of this book is a reprint of the author's earlier article,
"*Sylvie* ou la pensée de Nerval" (275), the second, entitled "Nerval, Gautier
et la blonde aux yeux noirs," points out and shows the artistic development of
a myth that is present in Gérard's "Fantaisie," *Corilla, L'Alchimiste,* and
Piquillo and in Gautier's *Mademoiselle de Maupin* and *Le Capitaine Fracasse.*
In his very sound and interesting discussion of Nerval's and Gautier's "eternal
feminine," Poulet makes the following important distinction: "Chez Nerval, le
type aboutit à une catastrophe non moins grave que chez Gautier. Alors que,
chez ce dernier, le type se fige, se pétrifie, perd de sa vigueur et de son origi-
nalité par un excès de précision et de détermination, on peut dire que chez
Nerval, c'est l'aventure inverse qui arrive. Il se perd lui aussi, mais par l'efface-
ment final de toutes ses déterminations propres. Il s'évanouit . . . dans sa
propre grandeur" (p. 134).

277. Priestley, J. B. *Literature and Western Man.* London: Heinemann, 1960.
512p.

Chapter VII, "The Romantic Movement in France" (pp. 159–72), includes an interesting discussion of *Les Chimères* and of Nerval's influence on the Symbolists.

a. P. Ciureanu. *Studi Francesi*, IV (1960), 361–62.

278. Proust, Marcel. "A propos du 'style' de Flaubert." *Nouvelle Revue Française*, no. 76 (1 janv. 1920), 72–90.

Contains the influential statement, "Gérard de Nerval . . . est assurément un des trois ou quatre plus grands écrivains du XIXe siècle. . . ." In discussion of *Du côté de chez Swann*, Proust states that he discovered part of his poetic method (or "ce procédé de brusque transition") in Chateaubriand's *Mémoires d'Outre-Tombe* and in Nerval's *Les Filles du Feu*. Affirming his conviction that Gérard's insanity was merely "un prolongement de son oeuvre," Proust admires in *Sylvie* the very substance and artistic techniques we admire today in *A la recherche du temps perdu*. "Ce phénomène de mémoire a servi de transition à Nerval, à ce grand génie dont presque toutes les oeuvres pourraient avoir pour titre celui que j'avais donné d'abord à une des miennes: *Les Intermittences du Coeur*."

279. ———. *Contre Sainte-Beuve*. Paris: Gallimard, 1954. 446p.

Pages 157–69 contain Proust's famous evaluation of *Sylvie*.

280. Quennell, Peter. *Baudelaire and the Symbolists*. London: Chatto and Windus, 1929. 222p.

One of the first commentaries by an English author recognizing Nerval's artistic importance. See pp. 66–98. Critical attention is given only to *Sylvie*, defined by the author as Gérard's "halcyon story" (p. 78).

281. ———. *The Singular Preference*. London: Collins, 1951. 223p.

Pages 18–24 include a discussion of the literary influence of *Sylvie* on the Symbolists and on Proust.

282. Radcliff-Umstead, Douglas. "Cainism and Gérard de Nerval." *Philological Quarterly*, XLV, no. 2 (1966), 395–408.

Analyses of the *Histoire de la Reine du Matin* and other works reveal Nerval as a Cainite and show how the poet attempted (particularly in *Aurélia*) to reconcile his Cainism with a loftier faith. The author's theories are at times unconvincing, and one is struck by such statements as: "Cainism, the exalting of Cain as a wronged hero and not as an envious villain, is Nerval's contribution to French literature."

283. Rat, Maurice. "Gérard de Nerval." *Vie et Langage*, IX (1960), 73–75.

Studies the rhyme of "El Desdichado" and shows that Nerval was "le premier qui montre à la rime l'incantatoire puissance des *mots longs* et aussi des *mots clefs*. C'est par là qu'il fut un singulier, un inimitable rimeur."

284. Reymond, Berthe. "Le Mythe féminin dans l'oeuvre de Nerval." *Etudes de Lettres*, VI, no. 4 (1963), 246–69.

A carefully developed study of Nerval and the eternal feminine, around which "se cristallisent et s'ordonnent les croyances et les recherches mystiques du poète: doctrines ésotériques, mythes et légendes, rêves, souvenirs. . . ." The author acknowledges the general presence of the myth in all of Gérard's later works, but she virtually limits her specific analysis to *Sylvie* and *Aurélia*, the first of which serves as a basis for the fully developed myth of the second. Whereas in *Sylvie* the poet strives to eternalize his love (for Jenny Colon) by projecting reality into an obscure past, in *Aurélia* he deliberately turns his back "au monde extérieur et à ses décevantes apparences pour faire confiance au rêve seul." The concept of the theatre as "véritablement le symbole de l'univers nervalien" and the theme of the mask are considered as elements of reconciliation, whereby unity and multiplicity are synthesized to form equilibrium and "la femme réelle" becomes for the poet "la femme éternelle."

285. Rhodes, S. A. "The Friendship between Gérard de Nerval and Heinrich Heine." *French Review*, XXIII (1949), 18–27.

An important discussion of the friendly and artistic relationship between the two poets. Although there existed obvious differences in character and personality, Nerval and Heine remained steadfast friends from the date of the latter's arrival in Paris (May, 1831) until his death. While certain of Heine's topics were foreign to Gérard's personality, the two nevertheless enjoyed a profitable collaboration in the French version of *L'Intermezzo* and *La Mer du Nord*. Rhodes cites the only existing letter from Nerval to Heine and comments on Gérard's linguistic difficulties in German.

286. ———. *Gérard de Nerval (1808–1855), Poet, Traveler, Dreamer*. New York: Philosophical Library, 1951. 416p.

The only complete biography of the poet in English. It is generally well organized and comprehensive, although the viewpoint is at times overly romantic. All critical analyses are presented primarily in terms of autobiographical elements.
 a. G. Gille. *French Review*, XXVII (1953–54), 481.
 b. M. Gilman, *Romanic Review*, XLII (1951), 298–300.
 c. J. Hankiss. *Erasmus*, V (1952), 240–42.
 d. P. Quennell. *New Statesman and Nation*, LXI (1951), 596–98.
 e. J. Richer. *Revue d'Histoire Littéraire de la France* (1953), 246–48.

287. ———. "Gérard de Nerval's Unfinished Novel." *Romanic Review*, XXXV (1944), 299–306.

One of the few studies of Nerval's only novel, *Le Marquis de Fayolle*, which Rhodes considers "an imaginatively conceived work that bears on almost every page the stamp of [Gérard's] temperament." Two opinions of the author differ from those of Clouard and Marie: first, Gérard's portrayal of himself in the novel is not in the figure of the Marquis but in that of Georges, whose love for Gabrielle mirrors Nerval's love for Jenny Colon; second, Nerval left his *roman-feuilleton* unfinished not only because of financial pressure but because "he could write down only what he had lived through and could recollect." That this novel does not measure up to Gérard's best work may well be the fault of Edouard Gorges, who, after the poet's death, undertook to finish the novel and distorted the plot, characters, and tenor.

288. ———. "Note on Gérard de Nerval's *Octavie*." *Modern Language Notes*, LX (1945), 172–76.

Cites evidence to prove that the original version of the famous letter in *Octavie* (and the third letter in *Un Roman à faire*), presumably written to Jenny Colon in 1837, is not the manuscript in the Collection Spoelberch de Lovenjoul. Rhodes shows that the opera mentioned in the letter, Giovanni Pacini's *Buondelmonte*, was not produced in Florence until 1845, and "to speak of the letter in which Gérard refers to it as of 1837 is an anachronism."

289. ———. "Poetical Affiliations of Gérard de Nerval." *PMLA*, LVIII (1938), 1157–71.

Describing *Aurélia* as "a compendium of the substance and essence of future symbolistic esthetics," Rhodes attempts to establish links between Nerval, Baudelaire, Rimbaud, and Symbolism. ". . . Nerval was the first poet to have the genius . . . to make himself a 'voyant' by the method Rimbaud was to prescribe later."

290. Richard, J.-P. "Gérard de Nerval ou la profondeur délivrée." *Critique*, II, no. 93 (1955), 484–509.

See 292, Chapter I: "Géographie magique de Nerval," pp. 15–89.

291. ———. "Langage et race chez Nerval." *Cahiers du Sud*, XLIII, no. 331 (1955), 364–72.

A study of Nervalian poetic syncretism, which, according to the author, suggests more a type of "exchange" and "reciprocity" than a confused mélange of diverse subjects. Nerval's syncretic universe is divided into three areas: (1) *religious syncretism*, in which diverse beliefs, the truths of which are exchanged, create the poet's spiritual universe; (2) the "*femme syncrétique*," an opposing figure who adheres to "le syncrétisme sensuel"; (3) *syncretic literature*, which demonstrates the constant exchange and imitation of themes, images, and characters and which manifests "une seule oeuvre . . . ouverte elle-même sur le mystère d'un homme . . . et de son destin intérieur." An attentive study of *Aurélia*, *Sylvie*, and *Les Chimères* results in an admirable discussion of Nerval's syncretic vocabulary and the means by which the poet was able to define syncretically his "race."

292. ———. *Poésie et profondeur* (Nerval, Baudelaire, Verlaine et Rimbaud). Paris: Editions du Seuil, 1955. 249p.

In Chapter I, "Géographie magique de Nerval" (pp. 15–89), the author analyzes Gérard's poetic material in terms of a method previously expounded by G. Bachelard. In the effort to obtain permanence, Nerval wanted to "dévoiler l'être," which would involve total escape from the real world. This he hoped to attain both in "le voyage" and in the ideal feminine type (*bionda e grassotta*). Directly connected with this attempt is the poet's relationship with nature and its secrets: the sun, water, the warm colors of green and red, all aspects of nature vitalized by the mystic "feu." Only when the poet can render nature completely "familière" can he begin to create and discover. Nerval's whole poetic creation is constructed around this quest for personal identity in relation to nature. Once he has attained this identity, Nerval is able to

develop a spiritual permanence, which in turn creates a new active experience
in each of his works. Richard cites the "Mémorables" of *Aurélia* as offering
us the most definitive example of Nerval's success in obtaining this spiritual
permanence and total understanding of nature. He also sees in Nerval's language an "épaisseur amoncelée," thus a type of linguistic condensation that
leads to a gradual sedimentation of expression.
   a. R. Jean. *Cahiers du Sud*, XLIII, no. 339 (1957), 312–14.

293. Richelle, Marc. "Analyse textuelle: 'El Desdichado' de Gérard de Nerval."
   Revue des Langues Vivantes, XVII, no. 2 (1951), 165–70.

   Approaches the sonnet as a work of art complete within itself and not as a
   piece that must be broken down and deciphered. "Ce serait . . . trahir le
   poème, que de vouloir interpréter clairement le sens de ce que l'auteur lui-
   même a manifestement voulu incertain."

294. Richer, Jean. "L'Amitié de Nerval et de Papion Duchateau." *Revue des Sciences Humaines*. Fasc. 61–64 (1951), 289–93.

   Brings to light the figure of Pierre Nicholas Ferdinand Papion Duchateau, one
   of Nerval's first literary friends, to whom he addressed several letters concerning his theatrical activity and early poetry. The first of the letters reproduced by Richer (dated 1831) relates to Gérard's play *Le Prince des Sots*.

295. ———, éd. *Aurélia ou le rêve et la vie* [*et*] *Lettres d'amour* (édition critique).
   Paris: Minard, 1965. 359p. [Les Lettres Modernes.]

   A critical edition of both works, including commentaries and articles (at the
   end of the volume) by the editor, by F. Constans, M.-L. Belleli, J. W. Kneller,
   and J. Senelier. See 30, 31, 194, 195, 91, 96. The format is particularly
   attractive, with the established text printed on the left-hand page and the
   corresponding critical commentary on the right.
   a. J. Villas. *French Review*, XL, no. 2 (1966), 299–301.

296. ———. " 'Avoir des entrées': un inédit de Gérard de Nerval." *Nouvelles
   Littéraires* (29 mai 1958), 4.

   Reproduces a journalistic commentary by Nerval on the theatre and relates
   certain elements to *Sylvie* and parts of *Angélique*.

297. ———. "Une Collaboration Gautier-Gérard: l'étude sur Henri Heine signée
   de Nerval." *Revue d'Histoire Littéraire de la France*, LV, no. 2 (1955), 206–9.

   Reproduces part of the manuscript of Nerval's study on Heine and shows the
   extent to which Gautier corrected the text. It is furthermore noted that in
   March, 1848, Gérard probably used certain of Gautier's notes on Heine in
   the preparation of his own introduction to the study.

298. ———. *Une Collaboration inconnue: la description du Panthéon de Paul
   Chenavard par Gautier et Nerval*. Paris: Minard, 1963. 32p. [Archives des
   Lettres Modernes; Archives Nervaliennes, no. 3.]

   In this important pamphlet, Richer brings to light six articles by Nerval and
   Gautier that appeared in 1848 in *La Presse* and that describe in detail Paul
   Chenavard's intended elaborate murals for the Panthéon. Having produced

evidence showing that Gérard was the major contributor in the collaboration, Richer points out the amazing relationship between the subject matter of Chenavard's murals and that of certain works of Nerval: ". . . La description du 'Panthéon de Chenavard' offre le caractère d'une véritable somme des grands thèmes mythiques épars dans l'oeuvre de Nerval" (p. 7). Richer compares: the syncretic symbolism of Chenavard's paintings with that of the *Aurélia* (where the poet refers to "mon ami Paul"); the painter's figure of Apollon with Nerval's "Napoléonide"; and both artists' treatment of Neo-Platonic themes. After proving that Baudelaire, in his article of 1859 on Chenavard, did little more than paraphrase certain parts of Gautier's and Nerval's studies, the author concludes that "l'histoire des relations entre Nerval et Chenavard apporte un cas singulier d'influence réciproque de la poésie et de la peinture, en même temps que d'une belle et longue amitié" (p. 24).

a. A. DuBruck. *Romanic Review*, LVI, no. 4 (1965), 307–9.

299. ———. "Compléments au Tarot de Nerval." *Tour Saint-Jacques*, 13–14 (1958), 12–26.

Reinforcing his contention that "Refuser systématiquement de faire appel à l'alchimie, à l'astrologie et au Tarot pour expliquer Nerval, c'est se condamner à rester sur le seuil de l'oeuvre . . . ," Richer offers additional evidence of the poet's use of the Tarot's imagery. He demonstrates the significance of Arcanas VII ("Le Chariot"), XVII ("L'Etoile" — which influenced Nerval's *récit* of the flood in *Aurélia*), VIII ("La Justice" — influential in the composition of *Octavie*), XVIII ("La Lune" — related to Nerval's Pythagorean concept of the universe), XIX ("Le Soleil" — image of human fraternity), XX ("Le Jugement" — connected with the ultimate *salut* of *Aurélia*), and XXII ("Le Monde" — symbol of unity).

300. ———. "Documents concernant Nerval: Gérard de Nerval et la Révolution de 1830; Autour du théâtre de Gérard de Nerval." *Revue des Sciences Humaines.* Fasc. 91 (1958), 401–9.

The first part of this text reproduces and comments on two early poems concerning the Revolution of 1830 ("Le Peuple" and "Les Doctrinaires, à Victor Hugo") and one prose fragment thought to be part of Nerval's *Mémoires d'un Parisien*. The second part reproduces the legal censoring procedures followed with regard to the plays *Piquillo, Léo Burckart, L'Alchimiste, Les Monténégrins,* and *L'Imagier de Harlem.*

301. ———. *Gérard de Nerval.* Paris: Pierre Seghers, 1950. 223p. [Reprinted in 1953, 1957, 1960, 1962.]

One of the most important contributions to Nerval study, this book includes approximately one hundred pages of biography and critical commentary on numerous aspects of the poet's work, many illustrations, and an adequate "choix de textes" at the end. Stating that "l'on sait que l'épanchement du songe dans la vie réelle est à l'origine d'une partie importante de l'oeuvre de Gérard de Nerval" (p. 97), Richer considers at some length the various archetypes and symbols that make up the poet's mythical world. Emphasizing the presence of esoteric influences (the Tarot, astrology, Pythagoreanism, etc.)

in Nerval's work, the author suggests various levels on which the texts might be studied.

    a. J. Briscot. *Etudes Classiques*, XXII, no. 1 (1955), 125.

    b. *Critique*, no. 97 (1955), 483–509.

    c. C. Pichois. *Revue d'Histoire Littéraire de la France*, LVIII (1958), 404–6.

302. ———. "Gérard de Nerval devant la psychanalyse." *Cahiers de l'Association Internationale des Etudes Françaises*, no. 7 (1955).

A fairly thorough analysis of the psychological and psychoanalytical studies of Nerval, based on theories of Freud, Bachelard, and Jung.

303. ———. *Gérard de Nerval et les doctrines ésotériques.* Paris: Editions du Griffon d'Or, 1947. 213p.

Although Richer has modified and, in some cases, changed certain of his theories on Nerval's esotericism (primarily and most recently in his *Nerval: expérience et création* — 312), this volume remains the standard, most authoritative study on the subject. Stating that "ce sens de l'ésotéricisme . . . fut au centre de la vie et de l'oeuvre de Nerval" (p. ix), Richer demonstrates the influence of such figures as Dom Pernety, Creuzer, Kircher, l'abbé Terrasson, Quintus Aucler, and, above all, Court de Gebelin and Martines de Pasqually. Constantly referring to Nerval's texts, he points out and analyzes numerous esoteric subjects: the Cabala, the Tarot, Freemasonry, Arithmosophy, religious syncretism, the doctrine of reintegration, Manichaeism, Gnosticism, Cainism, etc. Attention is frequently placed on number symbolism in the poet's work. While Chapter VI offers an explication of the sonnets "El Desdichado" and "Artémis," the following chapters take up such themes and images as "le type de la mère," "la reine de Saba," and "la Descente aux Enfers." A valuable bibliography of occult and esoteric source material is included at the end of the volume.

    a. P. Arnold. *Opéra* (10 sept. 1947).

    b. A. Béguin. "Les Poètes et l'occultisme," *Une Semaine dans le Monde* (16 août 1947).

    c. M. Carrouges. "Révélations sur Rimbaud, Nerval, Sade, et René Char," *La Vie Intellectuelle* (mai 1947).

    d. H. Duchesne [Hunwald]. *Paru* (oct. 1947).

    e. R. Kanters. "Pour l'histoire de la poésie," *Gazette des Lettres* (17 mai 1947).

    f. J. Pommier. *Revue d'Histoire Littéraire de la France*, XLVII, no. 2 (1947), 181–82.

    g. A. Rolland de Renéville. "La Poésie et l'ésotérisme," *La Nef* (août 1947).

304. ———. "Gérard de Nerval et les oeuvres du Baron de Bock." *Revue d'Histoire Littéraire de la France*, LIII, no. 1 (1953), 95–97.

Pointing out first that Gérard never truly mastered any foreign language and thus usually resorted to other translations or adaptations of foreign works before attempting his own translations, Richer demonstrates the extent to which Nerval used certain translations of Baron de Bock (in the *Choix de poésies allemandes, Léo Burckart, Voyage en Orient*) and how he borrowed from them the word "ferouër" and his concept of the Queen of Sheba.

305. ———. "Gérard de Nerval et Sylvie." *Revue de Paris*, LXII, no. 10 (1955), 116–26.

Expressing the opinion that "*Sylvie, avec Aurélia, représente la somme de l'expérience nervalienne,*" the author devotes the first part of this excellent study to the events that led up to the composition of the work. Although certain of its elements seem apparent as early as 1849 in *Le Marquis de Fayolle* (Chapter X), Richer dates its composition between 1852–1853, suggesting that certain ideas were developing in the poet's original project, *L'Amour qui passe ou scènes de la vie.* He contends that *Sylvie* is not autobiographical and that it was perhaps initially intended to precede the longer *Aurélia.* Parts II and III of the article consider the structure and major themes of *Sylvie*, and the author distinguishes the three heroines, or the "Trois Vénus," as perhaps the most revelatory aspects of the work.

306. ———. "Le Luth constellé de Nerval." *Cahiers du Sud*, no. 331 (1955), 373–87.

In this exhaustive explication of "El Desdichado," Richer interprets each verse on a biographical, astrological (and astronomical), and general level. Much of the exegesis is based on Nerval's genealogical charts (photographically reproduced in the article), which, the critic feels, greatly help to explain the poem. He concludes that "*l'interprétation astrologique du sonnet lui restitue le sens qu'il comportait aux yeux de Nerval et nous révèle le système employé pour le construire.*" (cf. 317)

307. ———. "Nerval au théâtre." *Revue des Lettres Modernes*, VII, nos. 58–59 (1960), 361–65.

Almost the complete issue of this review is devoted to "Nerval, critique du théâtre," and it contains both Richer's preface ("Nerval au théâtre") to Vol. II of the *Oeuvres complémentaires* and extracts from *La Vie du Théâtre* (pp. 368–452).

308. ———. "Nerval dans la nuit du tombeau." *Mercure de France*, CCCXVI (1952), 473–82.

Pointing out the rapport between the alchemical enigma *D.M. Lucius Agatho Priscus* (inscribed on the ms. of "Artémis") and *Pandora* ("Ni homme, ni femme, ni androgyne") and their relationship with Gérard's unfinished *Comte de Saint-Germain*, Richer traces the signature to Nicholas Barnaud's Theatrum *Atrum Chemicum* and interprets it as the alchemical tomb of Aelia Laelia, and the Philosopher's Stone. ". . . Nerval place la formule D.M. (aux dieux manes) devant Lucius-Agatho-Priscus, et il fait donc du sonnet 'Artémis' le tombeau de l'auteur du monument, époux de la pierre qui n'est autre que l'Ariste, le philosophe-poète." "Mausole" of the "El Desdichado" manuscript is defined in terms of the Mausolus-Artemisia legend and the alchemical "soma-sema" (body-tomb) idea.

309. ———. "Nerval et le théâtre." *Nouvelles Littéraires* (29 mai 1958), 12.

Calls for a more critical investigation of Gérard's plays and particularly *Léo Burckart*, classified as a "grand drame romantique injustement méconnu." Richer reminds the reader that, as in Scarron's *Le Roman comique*, the poet's love for the theatre is reflected throughout his work and that his failure as a dramatist may well account in part for the tragic suicide. While such lost plays as *De Paris à Pékin* and *Une Nuit blanche* are probably of little merit, *Piquillo*, *Caligula*, and *L'Alchimiste*, written in collaboration with Dumas, are worthy of critical consideration.

310. ———. "Nerval et ses deux *Léo Burckart*." *Mercure de France*, CCCVII, no. 1036 (1949), 645–78.

Before reproducing the 1838 unpublished original version of *Léo Burckart* (pp. 654–78), the author comments on the importance of this play in Nerval's work, the difference between the original version of 1838 and that published in *La Presse* in 1839, the facts behind the censorship of the play, and the enthusiasm with which it was received by the critics. (cf. 115 and 319)

311. ———. "Nerval et ses fantômes." *Mercure de France*, CCCXII, no. 1054 (1951), 282–301.

A thorough study, based on Jung's method, of the various themes and archetypes in *Sylvie* and *Aurélia*. The author distinguishes in particular the image of *la Mère* and the theme of the *double*. Referring to Chapter XVIII of *Voyage en Orient* ("Les Vénus"), he discusses the significance of "la Vénus infernale," "la Vénus populaire," and "la Vénus céleste" ("Etoile" — Artémis), all of which appear in *Aurèlia*, *Sylvie*, and "Artémis" as various aspects of *la Mère*. Aurélia demonstrates the fusion of the two archetypes, "de l'amour de soi à la projection de l'amour sur une femme, guide et protectrice, Double du héros et symbole de son *anima*."

312. ———. *Nerval: expérience et création*. Paris: Hachette, 1963. 708p.

In this erudite thesis submitted for his Doctorat, Jean Richer proposes to "étudier en détail les opérations mentales et les transmutations artistiques qui, au cours d'une existence assez banale quant aux événements extérieurs, permirent à G. Labrunie de devenir . . . ce qu'il voulait être, c'est-à-dire Gérard de Nerval" (p. 11). Thus, the thesis (the result of many years of devoted research by the greatest *nervalien*) is a study of the creative process in terms of human experience. Dividing his work into two major parts (1. the study of pre-existing myths and 2. the study of personal myths), Richer includes biographical material only when it is relative and pertinent to the poet's creative process, the basis of which appears to be Nerval's esotericism. The major works (particularly *Aurélia*, "El Desdichado," and "Artémis") are closely examined, as are such important topics as the poet's mysticism and genealogy, the theme of the "Napoléonide," the dominant image of "la mère et les mères," etc. Preceded by an admirable (though poorly documented) bibliography and a good index, the numerous photographic reproductions of autograph material and esoteric documents are extremely valuable. One can safely say that this is the most important single study ever published on Gérard de Nerval.

    a. *Bulletin Critique du Livre Français*, no. 222 (1964), 531.
    b. R. Kanters. *Figaro Littéraire* (28 mai–3 juin 1964).
    c. J. Kneller. *French Review*, XXXVIII, no. 1 (1964), 122–24.
    d. G. Raillard. *Le Français dans le Monde*, no. 30 (1965), 47–48.

e. A. Viatte. *Revue de l'Université Laval*, XIX (1964), 69–70.

f. P. Moreau. *Revue de Littérature Comparée*, XXXVIII, no. 4 (1964), 617–22.

g. J. Roudaut. *Mercure de France*, CCCLII, no. 1218 (1965), 740–43.

h. R. Chambers. *AUMLA*, no. 22 (1964), 318–20.

313. ———. "Nodier et Nerval." *Cahiers du Sud*, no. 304 (1950), 364–71.

Points out numerous similarities between Nerval and Nodier's novel *La Fée aux miettes* (1832), the hero of which is a lunatic whose mistress becomes for him each night the ravishing Balkis, or Queen of Sheba. Referring primarily to chapters XXII and XXV of the novel, Richer concludes that Gérard found here his image of the legendary queen.

314. ———. "Notes sur *Aurélia*." *Cahiers du Sud*, XXVIII, no. 292 (1948), 433–45.

First pointing out that the major events taking place in *Aurélia* refer back to the period between 1839–1841, Richer presents certain important texts and notes by Nerval relating to the composition of *Aurélia*. Of special importance is Richer's discussion of the "Mémorables," which were not included in the first set of proofs of *Aurélia* and whose plan constantly changed from manuscript to manuscript. He furthermore emphasizes the importance of the variants to *Aurélia* and discusses, by individual chapters, their relationship to the meaning of the established text. Additions to and revisions of these theories will be found in 312.

315. ———. "Les Opinions de Nerval et l'illuminisme." *Mercure de France*, CCX, no. 1045 (1950), 61–69.

A brief study of Nerval's connections with such initiates as Considérant and Delaage.

316. ———. "Une Page inédite d'*Aurélia*: 'La Reine de Saba.'" *Mercure de France*, CCXVI (1952), 462–72.

Produces an unpublished fragment of *Aurélia* and attempts to explain Nerval's complex description of the Queen of Sheba. This fragment, containing a number of images that appear in *Les Chimères* (primarily that of "la Reine"), leads Richer to the conclusion that "à cette mère-épouse sacrée [la Reine de Saba], suprème fleur de son déséspoir, confondue avec l'Isis des anciens et la Sainte Vierge des Chrétiens, Nerval a donné le nom d'Aurélia."

317. ———. "Précisions sur le 'luth constellé.'" *Cahiers du Sud*, no. 349 (1959), 450–52.

Points out Chapter 10 of Lucian of Samosata's *De l'astrologie*, with which Nerval was undoubtedly acquainted, which defines the "Lyre d'Orphée" in terms of the planets in the solar system and their function in the Zodiac. Citing further Gui de Fèvre de la Broderie's *Trois livres de la vie de M. Ficin* (a treatise on astrological medicine that designates the "luth" as the human body marked by the position of the planets at the moment of birth), Richer contends that Gérard's "luth" signifies both the microcosm and macrocosm, or the "âme-corps." (cf. 306)

318. ———. "Restitution à Théophile Gautier de deux contes attribués à Gérard de Nerval." *Revue de Littérature Comparée*, XXXV (1961), 251–53.

Lists five short stories published in *La Charte de 1830* or *Le Gastronome* that are considered not to be by Nerval: *Le Souper des pendus, Fantastique, L'Auberge de Vitré, Cauchemar d'un mangeur*, and *Soirée d'automne*. The latter two are probably by Gautier, whose *La Cafetière* of 1831 bears close resemblance to the *Cauchemar d'un mangeur*. The biographical allusion (and the name of the hero: Théodore) of *Soirée d'automne* would, without doubt, suggest Gautier as the author. The style of the other three *contes* is simply not that of Gérard.

    a. P. Ciureanu. *Studi Francesi*, V, no. 15 (1961), 574.

319. ———. "Le Roman d'un drame: Nerval et *Léo Burckart*," in *Le Drame romantique*. Paris: Club des Librairies de France, 1957, pp. 489–502.

An enlightened commentary on Nerval's finest play, *Léo Burckart*, and one of the few critical attempts to stimulate interest in the theatre of Gérard de Nerval. *Léo Burckart* (1838), executed in collaboration with A. Dumas (who probably composed most of the original version), is classified as "une des meilleures pièces de l'époque romantique" (p. 502). Richer points out that the play's initial lack of success was due not only to censorship but also to the fact that Hugo's *Ruy Blas* opened at the Théâtre de la Renaissance the same year.

320. ———. "Romantiques français devant les sciences occultes," in *Literature and Science*. Oxford: Basil Blackwell, 1955, pp. 242–50.

In this short study of the esoteric doctrines of Nodier, Hugo, Balzac, and Nerval, the author states that of all the Romantics "Gérard de Nerval est peut-être celui chez qui l'expérience intérieure épouse le plus volontiers les voies et les formes de l'occultisme" (p. 247). As with Victor Hugo, the occult world suggested to Nerval a means by which he could explore more keenly the realm of dream; but unlike the other Romantics, Gérard discovered in the occult sciences a veritable explanation of his own personal destiny.

321. Ridge, George Ross. *The Hero in French Romantic Literature*. Athens: University of Georgia Press, 1959. 144p.

Discusses Gérard de Nerval as the mystic, the pathological hero (or *homoduplex*), and the visionary. Also included is a fairly lengthy commentary on symbolism in *Aurélia*.

322. ———. "Representative Ideas of the Deathwish in 19th-Century French Literature." *Kentucky Foreign Language Quarterly*, VII (1960), 147–55.

The author by no means demonstrates a full understanding of the poet in his effort to define the role of death in Gérard's life and work. Nerval's deathwish is discussed in terms of an uncontrollable masochism and mysticism, twin factors that ultimately overwhelmed the poet in suicide.

323. Rinsler, Norma. "Classical Literature in the Work of Gérard de Nerval." *Revue de Littérature Comparée*, XXXVII, no. 1 (1963), 5–32.

Certain of Nerval's works indicate that in his youth Gérard familiarized himself with Italian, Greek, Latin, German, Arabic, and even Persian! Rinsler supposes that his classical education — before the translation of *Faust* — was of the standard type, with emphasis on a number of the great Latin writers in addition to the Greeks (Lucian, Xenophon, Plutarch, and Aristophanes). Nerval's knowledge of classical culture added an extra dimension to his style and to his whole existence. He is viewed as perhaps the most "classical" of all Romantics, showing clear preference for Greek to Latin cultures. In *Promenades et souvenirs* he cites Ovid as one of his favorites, stating also that he was greatly influenced by Lucretius. He mentions Apuleius from time to time, but it is Ovid and Virgil who constantly stand out in his work.

    a. G. Franceschetti. *Studi Francesi*, XXI (1963), 573–74.

324. ———. "Gérard de Nerval: The Goddess and the Siren." *Philological Quarterly*, XLIII, no. 1 (1964), 99–111.

A continuation of the author's theories on Nerval's cyclothymia, this article suggests that Gérard's attitude toward women alternated in the same fashion as his reaction to his father and that, depending on his mood, woman was either to be trusted or feared.

325. ———. "Gérard de Nerval and Heinrich Heine." *Revue de Littérature Comparée*, XXXIII (1959), 94–102.

After general remarks on the relationship between the two poets, the author points out Heine's "Les Dieux grecs" as the source for the ice-fire character of Kneph in Nerval's sonnet "Horus."

326. ———. "Gérard de Nerval and Sir Walter Scott's *Antiquary*." *Revue de Littérature Comparée*, XXXIV (1960), 448–51.

Submits that Nerval read Montémont's 1830 translation of Scott's *The Antiquary* and that he found here both his material for *La Main de gloire* and the enigmatical inscription "Oelia Lelia . . . ," which he used as "Aelia Laelia" at the beginning of *Pandora*, "D.M. Lucius Agatho Priscus. Nec Maritus" on a manuscript copy of "Artémis," and again in its entirety in *Le Comte de Saint-Germain*. Rinsler feels that while Nerval may have consulted Barnaud's alchemical interpretation of the expression in his *In Epitaphium Aenigmaticon* (the source cited by Richer in 1952 — 308), it is more likely that he originally found the inscription in Scott's novel.

327. ———. "Gérard de Nerval and the Divinities of Fire." *French Studies*, XVII, no. 2 (1963), 136–47.

Using as her guide E. Kretschmer's *Physique and Character*, the author contends that Nerval was a victim of cyclothymia, a temperament characterized by the alternation of lively and depressed moods, as opposed to schizothymia. Gérard's attitude toward his father can be better understood if we study him as a cyclothyme. Nerval relates love (which the cyclothyme constantly searches out) in terms of heat images or images of warmth. Rinsler exemplifies in the poet's work how certain "divinities of fire" (particularly Adoniram and Antéros) express the attitude of Gérard toward his father and thus toward God. Whichever masculine force it might be, the poet always experienced a double reaction of rejection and acceptance, and these patterns of undefined emotion are symbolized artistically by the gods of fire.

    a. P. Cuireanu. *Studi Francesi*, XX (1963), 373–74.

328. ———. "Gérard de Nerval, Fire and Ice." *Modern Language Review*, LVIII, no. 4 (1963), 495–99.

Discusses the significance of fires and warmth throughout Nerval's work, particularly in *Aurélia, Voyage en Orient*, "Horus," and *Pandora*. Fire, which the cyclothymic poet felt was drawn from the combined force of many human souls, is a symbol of life, as opposed to cold, symbol of the death of the human spirit.

329. ———. "Gérard de Nerval's Celestial City and the Chain of Souls." *Studies in Romanticism*, II, no. 2 (1963), 87–106.

States that Gérard's tendency to embody all large conceptions in the concrete and the personal is apparent in his images of the Celestial City and the chain of souls (both in *Aurélia*), which signify the human family and its bonds of affection. "The concept of the family has an importance for Nerval which cannot be overestimated. All his cosmic ideas, far from being abstractions, can be referred to this central theme."

330. ———. "Nerval and 'Aelia Laelia.' " *Revue de Littérature Comparée*, XXXVII (1963), 97–98.

Qualifies her comments in 326 by pointing out F. M. Misson's *Nouveau Voyage d'Italie* as the probable source for the expression "Aelia Laelia."
   a. G. Franceschetti. *Studi Francesi*, XXI (1963), 574.

331. ———. "Nerval et Biron." *Revue d'Histoire Littéraire de la France*, LXI, no. 3 (1961), 405–10.

"Biron" represented for Nerval (in "El Desdichado") a composite idea of all the heroic Byrons: the three great Biron leaders (a crusader, a great soldier of the sixteenth century, and a general during the Revolution), famous for their valor, adventure, and success in love. The author suggests that the key to this interpretation might lie in Nerval's study of Heine, where Byron is called the "fils de soleil," the solar archetype of the adventurous, gay, and virile hero. She furthermore sees "Lusignan et Biron" as Eros and Apollo, or nonfire and fire.
   a. *Studi Francesi*, XVI (1962), 172.

332. ———. "Nerval, Méry et deux pièces perdues." *Revue d'Histoire du Théâtre*, XVI, no. 1 (1964), 47–49.

Argues convincingly that the two supposedly lost plays of Nerval and Méry, *La Nuit blanche* and *Paris à Pékin*, are one and the same; that *La Nuit blanche* was the title that was ultimately applied to the original *Paris à Pékin*.

333. Roditi, Edouard. "Memory, Art and Death: Proust and Nerval." *Quarterly Review of Literature*, I, no. 3 (1944), 188–97.

A very sound and valuable article, which, while displaying a full understanding of both Proust's and Nerval's poetic experience, retains the merit of being the only study devoted exclusively to the artistic relationship between the two authors. Quoting liberally from *Le Temps retrouvé, Aurélia*, and *Sylvie*, the author demonstrates in the works the narrative device of involuntary memory or unconscious association through memory. "Unconscious memory, by pointing out analogies in time and experience, [played] in Proust's life, or in that of the fictional 'I,' the same part as dreams did in Nerval's life." On the other hand, there exist certain fundamental differences between Nerval's experience and that of Proust. Unlike Proust, who never confused the worlds of reality and dream and was thus able in the work of art to resolve his conflicts, Gérard tried to substitute dreams for life, finding ultimate escape not in art but in self-inflicted death. "For Proust, the real material event in the past becomes . . . revived and transfigured by memory when some analogous but less real and . . . less ideal experience in the present reveals the otherwise elusive substance which these two accidental manifestations have in common. It is this quality of realism which . . . drove him to seek concrete achievement in art rather than the more transcendental dreams which misled Nerval, through bright illusion and dark disillusionment, to final suicide."

334. Rolland de Renéville, André. *L'Expérience poétique.* Paris: Gallimard; Neuchâtel: Editions de la Baconnière, 1938.

A general discussion of certain metaphysical and spiritual poetic phenomena in modern French poetry from Nerval to Breton. Of particular interest is the chapter entitled "Le Sens de la nuit," which contains both a discussion of Nerval and Novalian "Présence" and a valuable interpretation of the sonnet "Artémis," "qui ne prend tout son sens que confrontée avec les premiers enseignements de la Kabbale sur les nombres" (p. 79).

335. ———. "Le Sens de la nuit." *Nouvelle Revue Française* (novembre 1936).
See 334, pp. 78–84.

336. ———. *Univers de la parole.* Paris: Gallimard, 1944. 244p.

A chapter entitled "A Propos des *Filles du Feu*" (pp. 9–20) classifies Nerval as the first figure in French literature to "introduire . . . une logique dont les aphorismes composent une synthèse des lois de l'esprit à l'état de veille, et de celles de la conscience endormie" (p. 10). After emphasizing the profound influence of the eighteenth-century Illuminists, the author depicts three major themes in *Les Chimères* and *Les Filles du Feu*: "épisodes vécus par le poète et prolongés par les événements de ses rêveries, l'emploi de symboles chers aux Illuminés, et les allusions aux religions antiques" (pp. 19–20).

337. Rouger, Gilbert. "En Marge des *Chimères.*" *Cahiers du Sud*, XXVIII, no. 292 (1948), 430–32.

Finds the source of the "Soleil noir" of "El Desdichado" in Heine's poem from *Le Livre des chants (Buch der Lieder)* entitled "Le Naufragé," which Nerval translated in 1848. He also points out the same image in Hugo's "Ce que dit la bouche d'ombre" and Proust's *Du Coté de chez Swann*. The "vieille romance" and "chanson d'amour" of the sonnet "Delfica" were perhaps borrowed from Goethe's *Second Faust*, and the "vautour" in "A Mme Aguado" more than likely refers to the Malasian *pantoum*. Rouger also shows how Nerval might well have made use of Francisque Michel's *Choix des poésies orientales* (1830).

338. ———. "Gérard de Nerval à Cythère." *Revue d'Histoire Littéraire de la France*, XLVIII, no. 4 (1948), 296–308.

Discusses the meaning and importance of Cythera (or Cerigo) in Nerval's mythical universe. This author shares the opinion that Gérard, in his description of the island in *Voyage en Orient*, depended more on the observations of others (for example, G.-B. Depping, Antoine Sériès, etc.) than on his own, and he demonstrates the parallels between Nerval's descriptions and those of other poets and geographers. He concludes that the island did not furnish Gérard the ideal image of ancient Greece he so wanted and that "c'est au pays de son enfance qu'il a vu Cythère, auprès des étangs de Loisy où sommeillent les eaux de la Nonette et de la Thève."
   a. S. Pappas. "L'Escale de Cythère? Un Plagiat de G. de Nerval." *Le Messager d'Athènes* (29 mars 1949).

339. ———. "Le Roman d'un voyage." *Nouvelles Littéraires* (29 mai 1958), 9.

In the *Voyage en Orient*, which Rouger classifies as "une 'revie' qui colore d'un jour nouveau le temps perdu," we find the very essence of Nerval's romantic personality and artistic abilities. However, Rouger sees the work more as "un voyage au long cours à travers les bibliothèques" than as a series of real and personal impressions. Particularly in *Les Amours de Vienne* and *Les Femmes du Caire* we sense the presence of Goethe, Hoffmann, Byron, Carlo Gozzi, William Lane, and, above all, Sterne. Rouger notes that Gérard's "ferouër" designates, in the real sense, not "double" but "une divinité femelle de la troisième catégorie." He further links Gérard's use of hashish with that of Dantès in Dumas' *Comte de Monte-Cristo*, which appeared shortly before the *Histoire du Calife Hakem*.

340. Salvi, Elvira. *Nerval*. Brescia: Morcelliana, 1945. 210p. [Reprinted in 1947.]

The outstanding biography of the poet in Italian. A fairly comprehensive bibliography is included on pp. 201–10.

341. Samaran, Charles. *Paysages littéraires du Valois. De Rousseau à Nerval.* Paris: Klincksieck, 1964. vii + 80p.

A handsome book and model presentation of literary geography. Of the three chapters on the Valois country, the first concerns Rousseau and Ermenonville, while the last two are devoted to Nerval, Châalis, and Les Hameaux. Included are 36 well-chosen illustrations.

342. Schaeffer, Gérard. "Sur le texte du *Voyage en Orient* de Nerval." *Revue d'Histoire Littéraire de la France*, LXIV, no. 2 (1964), 283–90.

Basically a commentary on Gilbert Rouger's critical edition of what this author calls "l'oeuvre maîtresse de Nerval." A number of new variants are cited, along with corrections and suggestions concerning the establishment of a proper edition.

343. Schneider, Marcel. "En Allemagne avec Nerval." *Nouvelles Littéraires* (17 août 1961), 6.

Traces with precision the German places, figures, and events described by Nerval in the *Lorely*.

344. ———. " 'Il y a longtemps que minuit a sonné.' " *Nouvelles Littéraires*
(29 mai 1958), 1–2.

In the form of a letter that Nerval might have written from Weimar, August 28,
1850, the author traces Gérard's German "heritage," emphasizing the impor
tance of the music of Schubert, Liszt, and Wagner in the poet's dream world

345. ———. "Nerval et la musique." *Tour Saint-Jacques*, 13–14 (1958), 60–64.

Although Nerval submitted articles on music to *Le Messager*, *La Presse*, and
L'Artiste from 1838–1844, and although he was one of the first to appreciate
the creative power of Liszt and the genius of Wagner, he still never expressed
a profound sympathy for the serious music of his day, particularly for the
popular Italian opera. Schneider attributes this conclusion to the fact that
Gérard was unable to find in formal music the "mystère" of the *chanson
populaire*: "Nerval préfère une naïve chanson populaire du Valois ou de
Beauvaisis. Ce sont ces airs de folklore qui ont imprégné son enfance: ce
sont eux aussi qui ont formé son sens musical et son sens poétique."

346. Schneider, Pierre. "Nerval ou le devoir de pureté." *Mercure de France*,
CCCVII, no. 1036 (1949), 689–97.

Discusses Nerval's poetic experience in terms of his moral and spiritual obligation, the "Faute" which, for the poet, could only be resolved in the work
of art. Gérard sought purification by such means as alchemy, but in the end
"pour Nerval, la littérature c'est le salut." *Sylvie*, *Les Nuits d'octobre*, "El
Desdichado," "Myrtho," and "Delfica" represent various stages in this spiritual quest for purity, and in *Aurélia* all conflicts are resolved: ". . . Tout est
consigné, voyage et port, purification et pureté, la Trame et les macérations."

347. Schukl, Pierre-Maxime. *Imaginer et réaliser.* Paris: Presses Universitaires
de France, 1963.

"Le Merveilleux chez Gérard de Nerval" (pp. 84–96) is one of the subjects
of investigation in Chapter V. Stating that "Nerval est un de ceux qui ont
réintroduit dans la littérature française le goût du merveilleux et du fantastique" (p. 84), the author (who leans heavily on Castex — 61) comments on the visionary and fantastic elements in such works as the "Vers
Dorés," "La Reine des Poissons," *Aurélia*, *Sylvie*, and *La Main de gloire*.

348. Sébillotte, L.-H. *Le Secret de Gérard de Nerval.* Paris: José Corti, 1948. 276p.

An extremely controversial study that places Nerval's "impuissance sexuelle"
at the center of his neurosis and mental conflict. The author establishes two
levels of psychological interpretation: (1) mythical: that Gérard sought
without success to fuse the figures of Jenny Colon and Marie Pleyel with the
sacred image of his dead mother; (2) biographical: that Gérard refused to
identify himself with a man (his father) whom he saw as both a hero and a
cruel, sadistic individual who possessed and virtually killed the mother
Gérard had never known. Nerval's "échec sexuel" is viewed as that of an
adult, resulting from an accumulation of childhood experiences. Although
certain of the author's ideas are thought-provoking, many of his theories are
far-fetched and implausible, such as the contention that Nerval demonstrated
on occasion incestuous inclinations. Furthermore, Sébillotte tends to concern

himself more with minute biographical detail than with the poet's work, although *Aurélia* does receive adequate attention. Most readers will agree that a closer investigation of Nerval's work would modify considerably the author's thesis. (cf. 229)

    a. C. Mauron. "Nerval et la psychocritique," *Cahiers du Sud*, XXXVI, no. 293 (1949), 76–97.

    b. J. Richer. *Revue d'Histoire Littéraire de la France*, II (1951), 210–12.

349. Sempoux, André. "Nerval et Dante." *Revue de Littérature Comparée*, XXXV (1961), 254–58.

Criticizing Marie-Luisa Belleli (32) for not having dealt in more detail with the influence of Dante on Nerval, the author contends that "la forme d'amour que Gérard trouvait traduite poétiquement dans la *Vita Nuova* et la *Commedia* rejoignait sans peine sa mythologie personnelle." Although Gérard's philosophy of love as expressed in *Aurélia* appears to have come under the direct influence of Dante ("l'idée d'une Beatrice-idéal"), Sempoux questions whether or not the poet may have found his ideas in German literature and especially *Faust*, where Dantean elements predominate. (cf. 364)

350. Senelier, Jean. *Un Amour inconnu de Gérard de Nerval.* Paris: Minard, 1966. 266p. [Les Lettres Modernes.]

Points out the hitherto unknown figure, Esther de Bongars, and discusses the role this actress played in Gérard's sentimental life. After presenting a well-documented biography of Esther, the author brings to light the single testimonial of Gérard's love for the actress: *Souvenirs d'un jeune premier*, written by the actor Adolphe Laferrière. Not published until 1884, this document contains the following phrase: "Qui n'a connu ses singulières amours [celles d'Esther] avec ce poète, ce mystique, ce fou charmant Gérard de Nerval." The entire investigation leads M. Senelier to study the many traits of Esther evoked by Nerval in such works as *La Pandora* and "Myrtho." The book is nicely illustrated by two engravings and sixteen plates, most of which deal with Esther and her career.

    a. M. Françon. *French Review*, XL, no. 5 (1967), 713–14.

351. ———. *Gérard de Nerval: essai de bibliographie.* Paris: Nizet, 1959. 349p.

This admirable bibliography, the most valuable tool to date for the study of Gérard de Nerval, contains 1,257 listings of primary bibliography and 1,222 secondary items. An introduction of 49 pages draws perspective on various problems in Nerval research and makes numerous suggestions as to which works and aspects of the poet especially merit further investigation. A short critical commentary preceding the "Bibliographie nervalienne" traces very generally the evolution of Nerval scholarship, from the poet's death to 1959. The short section at the end on iconographical documents is followed by both author and title indexes.

    a. P. Cuireanu. *Studi Francesi*, V, no. 13 (1961), 175.

    b. M. Françon. *Romanic Review*, LV (1964), 62–63.

    c. R. Jean. *Revue d'Histoire Littéraire de la France*, LXV, no. 3 (1965), 531–32.

    d. J. Voisine. *Information Littéraire* (1962).

352. ———. *Gérard de Nerval: recherches et découvertes (biographie, biblio-graphie et corrections à Pandora).* Paris: Minard, 1963. 40p. [Archives des Lettres Modernes; Archives Nervaliennes, no. 4.]

In this short pamphlet, Senelier touches on five different subjects: Nerval's position and journalistic duties at the *Figaro* between 1836 and 1838; the poet's text describing a statuette by Carle Elschoet; the theatrical career of Jenny Colon (including a chronological listing of her roles between 1822–1840); explanations of the "pas du shall," the "Je suis rchinka," the "costume des plus légers," the "Marta," the "apprendre le rôle de la Vieille," and the colors "pourpre" and "rouge" in *Pandora*; the influence of Alexandre Weill on Nerval (with a text by Weill entitled "Lettres fantastiques de l'amour et de l'amitié," which clears up the enigma of Nerval's letter of 1846 to Marie Pleyel).

    a. A. DuBruck. *Romanic Review,* LVI, no. 4 (1965), 307–9.

    b. *Revue d'Histoire Littéraire de la France,* LXV, no. 2 (1965), 331.

353. ———. " 'Pérégrinus' et la Traversée du Feu." *Tour Saint-Jacques,* 13–14 (1958), 74–77.

Interprets the meaning of the name "Pérégrinus," which Nerval used as a pseudonym for his *L'Ane d'or* and which appears in his comic opera *La Poly-gamie est un cas pendable,* in the *Carnet du Voyage en Orient,* and in *Sylvie.* The appellation, originated by Lucian of Samosata, was connected with the adepts' practice of walking on fire. Senelier contends that "la Traversée du Feu par Pérégrinus conduit Gérard de Nerval à considerer l'*élément* lui-même" and that the linking of Pérégrinus and Apulée attributed to "le triomphe final de l'Adept maître des épreuves qu'il a subies."

354. ———. "*Portrait du Diable* est bien de Nerval." *Revue de Littérature Com-parée,* XXXV (1961), 253–54.

Rejects W. T. Bandy's conjecture (14) that *Portrait du Diable* is a transla-tion or adaptation from an English original and points out an article of 1839 in *La Presse* in which are announced two short stories, *Raoul Spiphame* and *Un Mariage anglais,* by the author of *Léo Burckart,* M. Gérard. . . . The author notes that the subject of *Un Mariage anglais* is simply a first version of *Portrait du Diable.*

    a. P. Ciureanu. *Studi Francesi,* V, no. 15 (1961), 574.

355. ———. "Sylvie ou le bonheur perdu." *Nouvelles Littéraires* (29 mai 1958), 8.

A very lucid interpretation of the figure of Sylvie, "symbole d'une situation affective antérieure que Gérard désire de toute son âme ressusciter pour con-jurer les périls dont il est menacé." Sylvie, "la douce réalité," unable to reassure Gérard of his spiritual ideal (Adrienne, "le bonheur passé"), repre-sents for the poet the second and final phase of "le bonheur perdu."

356. ———. "Trois apocryphes de Gérard de Nerval." *Revue d'Histoire Littéraire de la France,* LV, no. 2 (195), 209–21.

Pointing out first that "Gérard de Nerval n'a signé et publié lui-même que trois écrits dont il n'est vraiment pas l'auteur: *Jemmy, Emilie,* et *Le Roi de Bicêtre,*" the author examines three other titles included in A. Marie's bibliography (no. 69: *Complainte sur la mort* . . . ; no. 73: *Complainte sur l'im-mortalité de M. Friffant*; and no. 49: *Nos adieux à la Chambre des Deputés* . . .) and concludes that these are not by Nerval.

357. Siciliano, Italo. *Romanticismo francese. Da Prévost ai giorni nostri.* Venezia: La Goliardica Editrice, 1955.

In his review of this book (not available to me), Mario Matucci states (in *Studi Francesi*, II [1958], 457–60): "Con un equilibrio sostenuto, senza indulgere in pericolosi sconfinamenti esoterici, ma considerandoli nel loro quieto valore, egli traccia un ritratto dolorosamente umano della tragedia nervaliana attraverso l'universo misterioso di *Sylvie* e di *Aurélia* e l'analisi di alcuni sonetti delle *Chimères*, culminanti nella desolata vedovanza di 'El Desdichado'" (p. 459).

358. Simches, S.-O. *Le Romantisme et le goût esthétique du XVIIIe siècle.* Paris: Presses Universitaires de France, 1964.

Contains comments on Gautier's and Nerval's attraction to eighteenth-century esthetic principles and especially to those of such artists as Watteau and Fragonard. Includes 20 well-chosen illustrations.

359. Smith, James M. "Gérard de Nerval." *Emory University Quarterly*, IX (1953), 157–66.

Analyzes the theme of the eternal Feminine in *Aurélia* and discusses Nerval's influence on the Symbolists and Surrealists.

360. Soccane, Pierre, and George Chase. "Jenny Colon, the Somber Star." *Musical Quarterly*, XXVI (1940), 76–86.

See 74.

361. Stambak, Dinko. "La Complainte de la noble femme d'Asan-Aga ou l'invitation romantique au voyage illyrien." *Revue de Littérature Comparée*, XXII (1948), 296–303.

Suggesting the influence of Yugoslav poetry on Gautier, Mérimee, Borel, Nerval, and others, the author notes the popularity of the "noble femme d'Asan-Aga" legend and also how it possibly suggested to Gérard certain ideas for the play *Les Monténégrins*.

362. Stout, Harry Linville. "French Translations of *Faust II*." *Kentucky Foreign Language Quarterly*, VIII (1961), 209–14.

Sees Nerval's 1840 translation of *Faust II* as by no means superior to those of Benôit, Arnoux, Lichtenberger, Chastenay, and others. One would question this judgment and also Stout's negative opinions as to Gérard's "deficient" understanding of Goethe's poem!!

363. Strauss, Walter A. "Gérard de Nerval." *Emory University Quarterly*, XXI, no. 1 (1965), 15–31.

In this beautifully written account of Nerval's poetic experience, the author states "[Gérard] is the only French Romantic who profoundly understood, and suffered from, the Romantic separation of man from world, and of rational self from mystical self; and going as far as he did in an attempt to bridge these gaps, he illustrates better than perhaps anyone else the hazards of the Romantic-Orphic alchemical quest for reintegration." Included are perceptive analyses of *Aurélia*, "Delfica," "El Desdichado," and "Artémis."

364. ———. "New Life, Tree of Life: The *Vita Nuova* and Nerval's *Aurélia*." *Books Abroad (Special Issue): A Homage to Dante* (May, 1965), 144–50.

A welcome and attentive comparative study of Dante's *Vita Nuova* and Nerval's *Aurélia*. Although the works show numerous parallels and similarities and both express the same general intentions, Dante's analogical vision in the *Vita Nuova* was not sufficient for Nerval, whose symbolic, Orphic vision of the cosmos (like that of Novalis) was made comprehensible only by means of the occult. "In the *Vita Nuova* all the signs are in the long run readable and comprehensible; in *Aurélia* certain signs are either deliberately misread, or no longer decipherable." (cf. 349)

365. Strentz, Henri. *Gérard de Nerval, son oeuvre*. Paris: Editions de la Nouvelle Revue Critique, 1933. 89p.

In this short biography of the poet, the author attempts to view Nerval through his work. Of the many biographical studies before 1940, this contribution is one of the few to break away from the Nerval "legend" and to recognize the genius in the poet's work, which, Strentz comments, wins "chaque année de nouveaux et plus attentifs lecteurs" (p. 76).

366. Sullivan, Dennis G. "The Function of the Theater in the Work of Nerval." *Modern Language Notes*, LXXX, no. 5 (1965), 610–17.

This important but generally neglected topic is discussed here in the light of *Sylvie*, *Aurélia*, and *Le Prince des Sots*. The true significance of the theatre in Nerval's work is metaphysical: ". . . Its function is that of a spiritual instrument which is concretely employed in [the poet's] quest." Nerval's artistic transformation of the world into a theatre allows him to define the correspondence between the two realms of human experience, and it gives depth to both the temporal and eternal mode of existence. In *Sylvie*, this theatre, which is used to bridge the incarnation of the real and ideal woman, is actually lived; in *Aurélia* and *Le Prince des Sots*, the theatre takes on a religious sense (a place of "épreuve"), evoking "the conception that [Gérard's] earthly experience is itself a penance which he must undergo to merit immortality."

367. Susini-Constantini, Hélène. "Gérard de Nerval et l'expérience du Temps." *Revue de la Méditerranée*, XVIX (1959), 399–410.

Whereas in his early work Nerval pretended to *dominate* the enemy time, his later works attest to the fact that he gradually began to *adhere* to the time element, adjusting his own personal experience to an unchanging force. Unlike Proust and more like Baudelaire, Gérard was never able to discover a perfect means by which memory could totally stabilize the happiness of the poet and guarantee bliss in the future: ". . . les minutes du souvenir où l'existence se révèle dans son intégralité, s'accompagnent rarement de la joie exaltante qui envahit l'être tout entier." However, like Baudelaire, Nerval was able to transform certain elements of the past and gradually create an eternal present, "où les choses se modèlent au gré de la fantaisie, où le temps perd son caractère de sinistre échéance: c'est le rêve éternel." Though the poet is unable to conquer time in the personal sense, he succeeds in comprehending and adhering to a circular order of time, whereby humanity and nature become only "une vaste chaîne qui déroule infiniment ses anneaux dans le temps et dans l'espace."

368. Teichmann, Elizabeth. *La Fortune d'Hoffmann en France.* Paris: Minard; Genève: Droz, 1961. 288p.

Although pp. 198–200 contain references to Nerval's translations of Hoffmann, the author makes no attempt to discuss the literary influence of the German poet on Gérard, nor does she adequately evaluate the translations.

369. ———. "Musäus et le Barbier de Goëttingue." *Revue de Littérature Comparée,* XXXIII (1959), 411–14.

Referring to W. T. Bandy's article of 1948 (14), which revealed Nerval's *Le Barbier de Goëttingue* to be a translation of Robert Macnish's English tale of 1826, Teichmann notes that Macnish's tale is itself no more than a translation of a short story by Musäus entitled *Stumme Liebe.*

370. Tiersot, Julien. *La Chanson populaire et les écrivains romantiques* (avec 96 notations musicales). Paris: Plon, 1931. 327p. [Reprinted in 1936.]

A large part of this volume (pp. 49–139) is devoted to Nerval's significant role in the development of the tradition of the *chanson populaire* and the relation of this tradition to literature. The author also cites the twenty-seven *chansons* mentioned by Nerval in the *Chansons et légendes du Valois* and in the article of 1842 published in *La Sylphide* entitled "Vieilles ballades françaises," and he demonstrates how he was able to identify still other songs by studying fragments quoted by Gérard. (cf. 84 and 165)

371. Tuin, H. van der. "Les Voyages de Nerval en Hollande." *Revue de Littérature Comparée,* XXXV, no. 3 (1961), 387–400.

In this unique study of Nerval's two trips to Holland, the author, in discussion of the first excursion of 1844, is forced to rely on the details furnished by Arsène Houssaye, Gérard's companion. Of particular interest for the two travelers was the Exhibition of Modern Painting at Amsterdam, where the author of *Sylvie* became fascinated by two female portraits by the Venetian painter Natale Schiavoni. Gérard himself furnishes excellent details of the 1852 trip and particularly of the argument between him and the archivist Scheltema over Rembrandt. Tuin portrays Nerval as an intelligent defender of the painter, certain of whose works influenced him considerably.

372. Tuzet, Hélène. "L'Image du soleil noir." *Revue des Sciences Humaines,* Fascs. 85–88 (1957), 479–502.

Tracing this literary image through the nineteenth century, Tuzet relates Nerval's use of the *soleil noir* (in "El Desdichado," "Le Christ aux Oliviers," *Voyage en Orient,* and *Aurélia*) to his alchemical practices. Unlike Gautier, who first used the image in his poem of 1834, "Mélancolia," Gérard applied a cosmic sense to the black sun, whereby the image is inserted "dans un complex où se lient, indiscernables, les éléments cosmogoniques, mystiques, sentimentaux: complexe où les symboles puisés dans l'alchimie jouent le rôle de ciment." The black body of the heavens is not that of Dürer's angel but of Nerval himself, and around this basic symbol revolve many of the poet's other alchemical symbols.

373. Valeri, Diego. *Il Simbolismo francese da Nerval a de Régnier.* Padova: Liviana Editrice, 1954. 151p.

In this short sketch of the Symbolist movement in France, the author demonstrates to some extent (in the chapter entitled "Il Simbolismo di Nerval e di Baudelaire") the precursory influence of Nerval and Baudelaire on the later movement. "E certo . . . che in Gérard de Nerval e in Baudelaire . . . è dato di cogliere con una commozione che poi non ritroveremo più, il primo fremito, il primo battito d'ala della poesia nuova" (p. 30). Valeri notes that the Symbolists admired most in Nerval the musical quality of his verses and the poet's projection of the dream world: "I sogni ci rivelano la verità unica ed essenziale . . . come figurazioni simboliche di quella verità, divina e, per se stessa, indecifrabile" (p. 32).

374. Valéry, Paul. "Souvenir de Nerval." Preface to *Les Chimères.* Paris: Les Amis de la Poésie, 1944. [Also published as: *Au sujet de Nerval.* Paris: Textes Prétextes, 1944. 27p.]

An influential essay that contains the statement: "Depuis quelque trente ou quarante ans, on s'est mis à lire [Nerval], on le réédite, on sais par coeur ses meilleurs vers: on l'aime." Valéry discloses an honest appreciation of the poet (contrary to popular belief!) and finds in his works the anguish and despair of twentieth-century man: ". . . Son érudition composite, débordant toutes les limites critiques, joignait, comme de proche en proche, un *domaine d'incertitude* où les produits les plus séduisants et les plus étranges de la pensée universelle se combinaient en une sorte de *savoir fantôme*." (Cf. 237)

375. Vander Burght, Laure et Raymond. *Gérard de Nerval, le troubadour ensorcelé.* Bruxelles: Goemaere, 1954. 180p.

In this sketchy, oversimplified biography, based in great part on Nerval's correspondence, the authors state that their purpose was not to "faire de l'exégèse, mais bien de rendre hommage à un homme dont les oeuvres nous ont ravis" (p. 173). Except for slight attention aimed at Nerval's "amitiés belges," the biography offers few original ideas and is of little use to the serious *nervalien*.

376. Vaudoyer, Jean-Louis. "Une Amitié romantique: Gérard de Nerval et Théophile Gautier." *Revue des Deux Mondes* (15 mai 1962), 176–89.

Discusses the youthful fraternal relationship between the two poets of the Doyenné, how Gérard saw less and less of Gautier after the former became infatuated with Jenny Colon, and how Gautier believed in Gérard's suicide and not a possible assassination.

  a. *Studi Francesi*, XIX (1963), 178.

377. Veen, J. van der. "Autour des *Chansons et légendes du Valois* de Gérard de Nerval." *Neophilologus*, XLIII (1960), 90–115.

Using three different folk songs as the basis of his study, the author demonstrates how Nerval, in his descriptions of the songs and folk legends of the Valois, contributed significantly to the science of ethnomusicology.

378. Viatte, Auguste. "Mysticisme et poésie chez Gérard de Nerval." *Cahiers de l'Association Internationale des Etudes Françaises*, XV (1963), 79–85.

Comments briefly on the poet's relations with the Illuminists of his day and attempts to define his "itinéraire spirituel." Particular interest is shown in the influence of such figures as Eliphas Levi (l'abbé Constant) and Henri Delaage.

379. ———. *Les Sources occultes du romantisme: Illuminisme et Théosophie, 1770–1820*. Paris: Honoré Champion, 1928. 2 vols.

Little attention is devoted to Nerval and his occult interests. Pages 11 and 251 of Vol. I ("Le Préromantisme") and page 33 of Vol. II ("La Génération de l'Empire") refer simply to the poet's name.

380. Villas, James. "Gérard de Nerval and Racine's *La Thébaïde*." *Romance Notes*, VI, no. 2 (1965), 116–20.

Suggests certain lines from Racine's *La Thébaïde* as a possible source of the expression "Dans la nuit du Tombeau" from the sonnet "El Desdichado." A relationship is established between the two poets' use of the same expression, whereby it is concluded that "Toi" refers to Gérard's lost mother, his consoling ideal.

381. ———. "Present State of Nerval Studies: 1957 to 1967." *French Review*, XLI, no. 2 (1967), 221–31.

Offers as complete a critical outline as possible of the most interesting and significant studies to appear on Gérard de Nerval since the publication of Léon Cellier's *Où en sont les recherches* . . . (65) in 1957. Approximately eighty-five items are discussed. It is noted that criticism during the past ten years has by no means been limited to Nerval's major writings and that serious efforts have been made to show that his artistic talents extend into regions other than those of dream and esoteric literature. A number of ideas are suggested at the end regarding future possibilities in Nerval research.

382. Virolle, R. "Rêve et réalité chez Gérard de Nerval." *L'Ecole*, no. 17 (1955). A study of the sonnet "Myrtho."

383. Vivier, Marie de. *Gérard de Nerval*. Paris: La Palatine, 1963. 224p. ["Poètes maudits."]

The author investigates two major biographical aspects: the poet's mental derangement and the figure of Gérard's father, Dr. Labrunie. Gérard's "volonté" was always weak, but not his reason; he always remained a lucid figure. In her introduction, Vivier states that we should not apply the term "insanity" to Nerval's condition but should call it, rather, a state of "déséquilibre neuro-psychique." This illness is said to have been brought on primarily by Gérard's overindulgence in alcohol, "remède redoutable qui aggrava son mal" (p. 9). Vivier attempts to rectify the position of Nerval's father, who, though tyrannical and at times extremely impatient and unsympathetic toward his son, was full of sincere concern and affection for Gérard.

384. Volbertal, J.-H. *Ermenonville, ses sites, ses curiosités, son histoire*. Senlis, 1923. 92p.

Chapter XVI, pp. 119–80, is a fascinating discussion of the town's importance in Nerval's work, especially *Sylvie*.

385. Weber, Henri. "Explication de texte: Gérard de Nerval." *Année Propédeutique*, nos. 3–4 (1952).

A plausible explication of the sonnet "Artémis."

386. Weber, Jean-Paul. *Domaines thématiques*. Paris: Gallimard, 1963. 344p. ["Bibliothèque des Idées."]

Extends his application of the alchemical motif "l'Allumage du Feu" (387) to *Aurélia*, certain other sonnets of the *Chimères*, *Les Filles du Feu*, and parts of the *Voyage en Orient*. Weber further studies the theme of the *double* as it is related to fire imagery.
    a. *Bulletin Critique du Livre Français*, XIX, no. 4 (1964), 332.

387. ———. "Nerval et les 'mains pleines de feux.'" *La Table Ronde*, no. 135 (1959), 96–107.

Develops in a rather awkward fashion the themes "l'Allumage du Feu," "l'Allumette," and "le Feu" as they appear in *La Main enchantée*, "El Desdichado," "Myrtho," "Horus," and "Artémis." As a thematic device, the image of alchemical fire is best employed by the poet in *La Main enchantée*: "Il y a, somme toute, comme une *idée fixe* ou une obsession dans *la Main enchantée*, et c'est celle du Feu, de la flamme rouge qui détruit et consume."

388. Weise, Otto. *Gérard de Nerval, Romantik und Symbolismus*. Halle: Akademischer Verlag, 1936. 148p.

A valuable dissertation that first discusses Nerval's position and importance in the evolution of one literary period into another and, second, attempts to synthesize the various influences exercised on the poet by such German writers as Goethe, Hoffmann, Heine, and Schlegel. Minimum attention is devoted to biographical matters, and maximum concentration is on the primary works. Of particular interest is Chapter IV, in which the author points out and studies the close relationship between Nerval and Baudelaire. The excellent bibliography in the Appendix not only corrects and adds to A. Marie's bibliography of 1926 (221) but also includes a very useful listing of publications on Nerval in English.

389. Wettstein, Denyse. "Nerval et l'évocation du Valois." *Etudes de Lettres*, VI, no. 4 (1963), 230–45.

To understand fully the parallel between the realism and subjectivism of *Sylvie*, *Angélique*, and *Promenades et souvenirs*, one must study the detail of Nerval's representations of the Valois. The poet's descriptive method is characterized as follows: ". . . une succession de plans nettement dessinés qui se détachent les uns des autres; . . . une seule phrase [qui] décrit souvent l'ensemble du spectacle." Emphasizing the importance of geographical setting in all three works, the author distinguishes six major themes connected with the Valois: water ("qui contribue certes à donner un caractère de transparence à la province"), trees ("symboles de vitalité et de jeunesse, . . . éléments verdoyants du Valois"), light ("expression concrète du bonheur"), Chateaux ("symboles du bonheur; l'enfance et l'amour"), music ("représente l'idéal vers lequel tend nostalgiquement Gérard"), and social festivity ("évocateur de joie . . . d'un pays heureux"). The Valois becomes more than a frame-setting in which action takes place; it gradually comes to represent for Nerval a living force, a personage, playing a veritable role.

390. Whyte, Peter. "Gérard de Nerval, inspirateur d'un conte de Gautier, *Deux acteurs pour un rôle.*" *Revue de Littérature Comparée*, XL, no. 3 (1966), 474–78.

On Gautier's borrowings for his tale, which appeared in *Le Musée des Familles* for July, 1841, from Nerval's *Les Amours de Vienne* (*Revue de Paris*, March, 1841).

391. Wurmser, André. "Gérard de Nerval et le folklore." *Lettres Françaises*, no. 553 (27 janv.–3 fév. 1955), 5.

Such works as *Sylvie*, *Les Faux-Saulniers*, and *Chansons et légendes du Valois* were primarily the results of Nerval's knowledge and love of French and German folklore. Folk tradition (particularly in the form of *la chanson populaire* and *la danse populaire*) was for Gérard "un document précieux, une source d'inspiration."

Unpublished or Unfinished Doctoral Theses on Gérard de Nerval

392. Chambers, Ross. "La Poétique du voyage." Sydney, Australia, 1967.

393. Clerc, G. "Le Sourire de Nerval." McGill, in preparation.

394. Eder, Suzanne. "Mythische und Symbolische Elemente in den Dichtungen von Maurice de Guérin und Gérard de Nerval." Tübingen, 1949.

395. Glavin, M. "Gérard de Nerval." Berkeley, in preparation.

396. Greene, L. "Les Lieux privilégiés dans l'oeuvre de Nerval." Yale, in preparation.

397. Hefke, George W. "Chronologie de la vie et des oeuvres de Gérard de Nerval." *Dissertation Abstracts*, XXV (1965), 7268.

398. Hubert, Claire M. "The Still Point and the Turning World: A Comparison of Myths of Gérard de Nerval and William Butler Yeats." *Dissertation Abstracts*, XXVI (1965), 1042–43.

399. Ingler, James B. "Woman as Myth in the Works of Gérard de Nerval." *Dissertation Abstracts*, XXVII (1966), 1824A.

400. Koch, Melanie. "Die Bedeutung der Liebe in Leben und Dichtung von Gérard de Nerval." Tübingen, 1951.

401. Morris, Edward P. "*Aurélia* and Its Place in Nerval's Works." Harvard, 1955.

402. Osmond, N. H. H."The Imaginary Love-life of Gérard de Nerval." University of Keele, 1967.

403. Rinsler, Norma. "Gérard de Nerval: The Relationship Between His Writings and His Temperament." University of London, 1961.

404. Roeben, Ingrid. "Semantische Untersuchungen zum Theme Ernerung im Werk des Fränzosischen Gérard de Nerval." Tübingen, 1962.

405. Schaeffer, J. "Le Mythe de la création et du créateur dans le *Voyage en Orient*." Neufchâtel, Switzerland, 1967.

406. Sobby, Zenab. "*Les Femmes du Caire* de Nerval." Paris, 1955.

407. Wilhelm, Julius. "L'Idée de la mort dans les poésies de Gérard de Nerval." Tübingen, in preparation.

Index

ABOUT THE AUTHOR

JAMES VILLAS has concentrated a great deal of attention for several years on the works of Gérard de Nerval and on the research this author has stimulated. He was able, while in France as a Fulbright scholar in 1961–1962, to study with the distinguished Nervalian, Léon Cellier, and in subsequent years he has carried out much of his work in close affiliation with other leading authorities both in Europe and in this country. In addition to his articles on Mauriac and on Petrarchism, his research on Nerval has been published in the leading literary journals. His "Present State of Nerval Studies: 1957 to 1967" appeared recently, in the November, 1967, issue of *The French Review*.

Professor Villas received his doctoral degree from the University of North Carolina in 1966 and is Assistant Professor of French at the University of Missouri, Columbia. At present, he is engaged in a book-length study of "The Poet's Exile in French Literature."